Composts and composting

The term 'compost' is often used mistakenly and can cause great confusion. The definitions for 'garden compost' and 'seed and potting composts' are given below. In addition, there are moisture-retentive materials that are added to potting composts, especially when plants are growing in small amounts of compost in containers. There are also specialist composts for some plants, such as bulbs (when potted for indoor display), orchids, cacti and ferns.

What is garden or plant compost?

GETTING THE TERMS RIGHT

Garden compost

Derived from putting organic waste material from gardens and kitchens onto compost heaps and into compost bins and allowing it to decompose so that it can be dug into the soil or used as a mulch (see pages 12–43 for details). It is an important yet inexpensive way of improving a soil's structure, as well as returning nutrition to it. Wormeries (see pages 48–53) are a further method of decomposing organic material. Compost can also be created in trenches and holes (see page 29). Green manuring (see pages 54–57) is another excellent way to improve soil. Normally, kitchen and garden waste takes about a year to decompose (the speed of decomposition depends on the time of year), but there is a 'quick composting' method (pages 30–31) that you can use.

Seed and potting composts

Used when sowing seeds in pots and seed-trays (flats), as well as when potting plants. These composts range in type and formulation and are mainly based on 'partially sterilized loam', 'peat-based', 'reduced-peat' or 'peat-free' materials (see pages 58–77 for details of these).

Using clean seed and potting composts ensures that seeds and seedlings can be given a good start in life.

Using waste organic material from kitchens and gardens to create garden compost is an important part of organic gardening.

CAN I USE GARDEN SOIL IN SEED AND POTTING COMPOSTS?

Compost in which seeds are sown and plants grown is specially prepared and formulated to ensure it is clean and free from pests and diseases; it also contains a balanced diet of plant foods. Its structure enables air to penetrate the mixture and excess water to drain away, yet it is still moisture-retentive. It is free from the seeds of weeds, which would cause radical problems if they germinate at the same time as the sown seeds.

Occasionally, garden soil or friable loam, with the addition of sharp sand, is used in very large patio tubs as a way to save money, but if soil pests are present they soon devastate roots and bring about the death of plants.

Organic gardening

What does organic gardening involve?

This is gardening without resorting to the use of pesticides and fungicides to control pests and diseases, and not using synthetic and non-organic fertilizers to feed plants. It also fundamentally embraces the use of organic materials, such as garden compost, that are derived from the decomposition of material from plants and kitchen waste, and dug into the soil or used as a mulch. It also involves good 'husbandry' of the soil (see below).

SOIL HUSBANDRY

Sometimes considered an archaic term, good soil husbandry embraces the traditional way of keeping soil healthy and productive, both for present and future generations. It includes annual winter digging of vegetable plots and seasonal flower beds (see pages 44–45 for the techniques of single and double digging). The benefits of digging are:

Enables decayed compost and manure to be dug in

It enables decayed garden compost and manure to be mixed into the ground (see pages 44–45).

Exposing larvae

It exposes the larvae of some soil pests, such as cockchafer grubs, to frost and birds.

Improving drainage

It improves drainage by breaking up the soil to a depth of 25–30 cm (10–12 in) for single digging, and about 60 cm (2 ft) for double digging.

Soil aeration

It improves soil aeration, which is essential for the activities of roots and beneficial soil organisms.

Buries annual weeds

It buries annual weeds (see pages 18–19 for descriptions and illustrations). Alternatively, they can be placed on compost heaps or in compost bins. Perennial weeds (see pages 22–23 for descriptions and illustrations) should neither be buried nor put in compost heaps and bins, but burned or put in a strong polythene bag to decay (see page 22).

OTHER GOOD SOIL HUSBANDRY TECHNIQUES

- Mulching soil (see page 47).
- Rotating crops (see page 46).
- Creating garden compost (see pages 12–43).
- Encouraging beneficial insects and creatures into gardens to help combat plant and soil pests (see pages 8–9).
- Making leafmould (see pages 10–11).
- Recycling kitchen and garden organic waste (see pages 6–7, and pages 14–25 for materials that can and cannot be composted).
- Creating a wormery (see pages 48–53).
- Green manuring (see pages 54–57).

Exposes soil to wintery weather

It exposes the surface to winter weathering that breaks down large lumps of soil and creates a friable tilth in which seeds can be sown in spring, and plants planted.

First published in 2009 by New Holland Publishers (UK) Ltd
London • Cape Town • Sydney • Auckland
Garfield House, 86–88 Edgware Road, London W2 2EA, United Kingdom
www.newhollandpublishers.com
80 McKenzie Street, Cape Town 8001, South Africa
Unit 1, 66 Gibbes Street, Chatswood, NSW 2067, Australia
218 Lake Road, Northcote, Auckland

ISBN: 978 1 84773 326 9

7 6 5 4 3 2 1

Direction: Rosemary Wilkinson Project Editor: Amy Corstorphine Production: Laurence Poos
ned and created for New Holland by AG&G Books Copyright © 2004 "Specialist" AG&G Books
gn: Glyn Bridgewater Illustrations: Dawn Brend, Gill Bridgewater, Coral Mula and Ann Winterbotham
r: Alison Copland Photographs: see page 80
roduction by Pica Digital Pte Ltd, Singapore
ted and bound in Malaysia by Times Offset (M) Sdn. Bhd.

The COMPOST

Specialist

The essential guide to creating and using garden compost, and using potting and seed composts

David Squire

Series editors: A. & G. Bridgewater

NEW HOLLAND

Contents

Author's foreword

Keeping garden soil in good health is an essential part of gardening. Unless the fertility of soil is maintained, together with its ability to encourage the healthy growth of roots through the presence of beneficial soil organisms, plants will never grow healthily. It also needs to be well aerated yet moisture-retentive. Keeping soil in good condition involves the regular addition of manure or decomposed organic material, such as garden compost. Obtaining farmyard or horse manure is difficult for most home gardeners, but organic waste from kitchens and gardens is readily obtainable and inexpensively converted into garden compost for digging into the soil or using as a mulch.

A major part of this abundantly illustrated book describes how to convert this freely available material into garden compost. There are also other ways to 'green' garden without using compost heaps or compost bins, such as digging fresh organic material directly into trenches or holes; all of these methods are explained in detail. Wormeries, where special worms are given the task of converting organic waste from kitchens and gardens into compost, are also described.

The range of composts in which seeds can be sown, seedlings pricked out and plants potted and repotted can be confusing. The advantages and disadvantages of each of these composts are described – whether 'loam-based', 'peat-based', 'reduced-peat' or 'peat-free' – and all have their devotees.

This detailed and thoroughly practical book guides you through the best methods of recycling kitchen and garden organic waste, as well as choosing or making your own composts for sowing seeds or potting up plants.

Measurements

Both metric and imperial measurements are given in this book – for example, 1.8 m (6 ft).

SEASONS

Throughout this book, advice is given about the times to tackle composting. Because of global and even regional variations in climate and temperature, the four main seasons have been used, with each subdivided into 'early', 'mid-' and 'late' – for example, early spring, mid-spring and late spring. These 12 divisions of the year can be applied to the appropriate calendar months in your local area, if you find this helpful.

IS IT COSTLY TO GET STARTED?

If you start with a compost bin made from old and abandoned materials, the cost is practically negligible. Proprietary compost bins are widely available, but old and abandoned items, such as plastic dustbins, can be quickly converted for use (see pages 36–37), while home-made types are well within the abilities of do-it-yourself enthusiasts (see pages 34–35). Preparing the soil beneath a compost heap or bin is important and this is discussed on pages 26–27.

If compost bins are not a possibility, especially in a small garden, organic waste can be buried directly in trenches or holes (see page 29). Leafmould is inexpensive to make and, apart from putting deciduous leaves (those that fall from shrubs and trees in autumn) into wire-netting enclosures, they also can be put in strong polythene bags and left to decay in out-of-the-way places in a garden (see pages 10–11).

In small gardens with insufficient space for a compost heap or bin, organic waste can be put in trenches or holes.

One way to create leafmould is to put leaves directly in a strong polythene bag.

IS 'GREEN GARDENING' SMELLY?

Although it involves the decomposition of organic materials from kitchen leftovers to garden waste such as annual weeds, old cabbages and lawn mowings, green gardening need not be smelly, nor cause problems for neighbours. If you put a compost heap or bin in an out-of-the-way position (see pages 26–27), there will not be a problem. You can also use a trellis or hedge to screen it from view.

Wormeries, which are usually positioned nearer to a house than a compost heap or bin, do not usually produce bad smells. Should this arise, however, it is easy to identify the cause and rectify the problem (see pages 48–49).

Green gardening becomes a way of life for many gardeners; it ensures that food grown in your garden is not contaminated with toxic chemicals.

WHAT ARE WORMERIES?

Worms that feed on vegetable waste are kept in specially constructed compost bins, often called wormeries. These worms eat about three times their own weight in food each week and turn it into compost for mulching the soil's surface or digging into the ground. For detailed information about wormeries and looking after them, see pages 48–53.

Wormeries are easy to look after and can quickly gain the attention and enthusiasm of all family members.

Recycling organic waste

How can I recycle organic waste?

In modern times, recycling organic waste from kitchens and gardens is seen as environmentally friendly. Yet it is also a natural way of gardening that has proved itself to be viable and trustworthy to many generations of gardeners, and is the best way to keep soil healthy and productive. Bacteria, fungi, insects and other creatures that keep soil healthy and fertile benefit from regular additions of decomposed garden compost, which is free and readily available.

Keeping soil free from toxic chemicals

With the increasing number of people this planet is expected to support, there is a constant need to make land more productive of food crops. This has led to increasing amounts of artificial fertilizers being added to the soil to produce larger crops. Inevitably, this has resulted in pesticides and fungicides being used more frequently to prevent plants becoming damaged and inedible. Eventually, soil can become so full of artificial chemicals that it is toxic to plants, with increasing seepage of chemicals into watercourses causing major pollution.

However, by adopting a policy of recycling kitchen and garden waste and turning it into material that can be returned to the soil, either through mulches or by digging it into the ground during autumn and winter, the soil in your garden can retain its natural integrity and become productive of wholesome crops.

Allotments, as well as gardens, are ideal places where organic waste material can be recycled to improve the soil for the following crops.

WHAT ARE THE BENEFITS OF ORGANIC GARDENING?

There are several benefits, including:
- **Saving money:** Composting organic waste will avoid you having to buy manure for digging into the soil both to enrich its nutritional value for plants, and to improve its structure (better aeration, drainage and moisture-retaining capabilities). It also encourages the presence of beneficial bacteria, fungi and soil creatures that help in the decomposition of organic materials.
- **Growing better crops:** If you improve the quality of soil, plants will grow more healthily. Whether vegetables and fruits taste better in soils regularly enriched organically, rather than given repeated applications of artificial fertilizers, is debatable but once you have tasted food grown in soil enriched with garden compost or manure you will probably be converted to organic gardening.
- **Improving the environment:** Mixing garden compost with the soil, or using it as a mulch, encourages the presence of insects and this leads to the increasing presence of birds and small mammals. Apart from enriching a garden with life, many of

these insects, mammals and birds help in the control of garden pests. A wide range of beneficial insects and creatures is described and illustrated on pages 8–9.

- **Healthy soil:** This is vital to plants, and where decomposed organic material has not been mixed into the soil for several years it becomes partially dead. Soil aeration is vital to enable roots to perform properly, moisture retention aids the growth of roots and activities of soil organisms, and good drainage prevents waterlogging, when both roots and soil creatures die. Garden compost and manure also provide plants with major nutrients, such as nitrogen, phosphates and potash, as well as many minor and trace elements.

- **Slow release of nutrients:** Garden compost and manure release nutrients slowly, especially if the weather is cool and plants are not growing rapidly, but more quickly during higher temperatures in summer, when growth is active. This is because the soil organisms that break down these materials are more active when the weather is warm. This is ideal for promoting well-balanced plant growth throughout the year. Most chemical fertilizers cannot achieve this slow and timely release of nutrients. Although slow-release fertilizers do release their nutrition in a timed-release manner, they still need to be applied at the correct time of year, in spring rather than in winter, when plants are dormant.

Flower borders benefit greatly from decomposed organic waste being mixed with the soil in order to improve its fertility and ability to support plants.

ELIMINATING THE NEED FOR A BONFIRE

In years gone by, a bonfire was a traditional part of gardening, especially in autumn and when thick, woody plants needed to be 'got rid of'. It also had the benefit of providing wood ash for mixing with the soil or adding to a compost heap. Wood ash contains variable amounts of potash, with hardwood containing 1–10 per cent potash, as well as 35 per cent calcium and 1.5 per cent phosphates. However, with the attention now given to atmospheric pollution, bonfires are not popular and they can be troublesome to neighbours. Nevertheless, a bonfire is an ideal way to get rid of the roots of perennial weeds, although they can also be put in a polythene bag to decay over a long period (see pages 22–23). Instead of burning woody waste, it can be shredded and used either as a mulch or added in limited amounts and in thin layers to compost heaps and bins (see pages 24–25).

REDUCING LANDFILL

For many decades, any rational person could have predicted that putting all rubbish into landfill sites was unsustainable – but it continued. It was also wasteful of this planet's resources. Nowadays, most local authorities have a more sensible policy and ask for recyclable waste (including newspaper, magazines, metal tins, glass and plastic bottles) to be put in one collectable bin, and landfill waste in another, which often includes organic waste (well wrapped) from kitchens. Better still, however, is to add all organic kitchen waste to compost heaps and compost bins (see pages 12–43), as well as in limited amounts to wormeries (see pages 48–53).

Beneficial creatures

Some insects act as predators or parasites on many garden 'pests', helping to prevent damage to plants without the need for chemical controls. Other beneficial creatures, such as frogs, toads, centipedes, hedgehogs, shrews, slow-worms and spiders, also play an important role in killing plant pests (see opposite page). Controlling plant pests in this way is increasingly popular, and a safe and sustainable way to protect your plants.

In what way are creatures beneficial?

BENEFICIAL INSECTS

Getting the terms right ...

• **Beneficial insects:** These are insects that help to control plant-damaging insects • **Biological (or natural) controls:** These encompass the methods for killing plant-attacking insects without chemicals • **Green gardening:** A term for growing plants without the use of chemicals to control and prevent pests and diseases, as well as for not using artificial chemicals to feed the plants or kill the weeds • **Organic gardening:** A popular term for controlling pests and diseases without resorting to the use of chemicals; however, it is a 'hijacked' term as all plants grow organically • **Parasites:** Usually, this refers to the young stages of parasites that live in or on the body of the plant being attacked • **Predators:** These are insects, as well as other creatures and animals, that roam around gardens, killing and eating plant-damaging pests.

Black-kneed capsid bugs

Adult

These bugs lay eggs on apple trees from mid-summer to autumn. They hatch, and the nymphs and adults reduce red spider mite infestations. Nymphs eat 5–40 red spider mites each day, while adults eat 60–70.

Dragonflies

Adult

These attractive insects (including damselflies), as adults, flutter over ponds. The nymphs live in ponds, dykes, marshes, canals and slow-moving streams. In both their nymph and adult stages they will eat other insects.

Green lacewings

Adult

Also known as 'green eyes', they lay batches of greenish eggs on stalks. These hatch, and the larvae eat mainly small aphids, sucking out their body fluids. Each larva eats many hundreds of aphids, as well as mites and leafhoppers.

Powdery lacewings

Larva
Adult

Smaller than green lacewings, they are covered in fine, white powder and resemble greenhouse whiteflies. In orchards, the larvae and adults feed almost entirely on red spider mites and their eggs. Each larva eats 15–35 mites per day.

Ladybirds

Larva
Adult

There are many species, with different colours and spots. Both larvae and adults are predators, eating vast numbers of aphids as well as mealy bugs, thrips, mites and scale insects. Each larva of the two-spot ladybird eats 15–20 aphids a day (up to 500 in a three-week larval stage).

Ground beetles

Adult
Larva
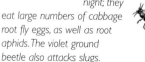

These are natural predators, with agile, well-armoured larvae. Both adults and larvae destroy large numbers of small insects, especially at night; they eat large numbers of cabbage root fly eggs, as well as root aphids. The violet ground beetle also attacks slugs.

Rove beetles

Large family of soil-living beetles, including the devil's coach-horse. Both adult and larvae rove beetles are predators and voraciously consume lettuce root aphids, strawberry aphids and red spider mites. Adult beetles completely devour mites, while larvae suck them.

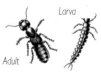
Larva
Adult

BENEFICIAL INSECTS (CONTINUED)

Ichneumon flies

Mainly parasites of moth and butterfly caterpillars; a few parasitize spiders, lacewings and aphids. Females have long egg-laying parts (ovipositors), enabling them to lay eggs in the bodies of their prey. Eggs hatch and the larvae eat the insect's body from the inside.

Adult

Braconids

Adult

Parasitical in nature, braconids attack many insects, laying eggs in the caterpillars of a wide range of moths and butterflies. They also attack aphids. The larvae of some braconids, when emerging from their host, build cocoons in a mass.

Chalcids

Large group of mostly parasitical flies that attack butterflies (especially white butterflies), moths (including ermine moths), flies and scale insects, laying eggs in their larvae. Chalcids are more beneficial to gardeners than either ichneumon flies or braconids.

Adult

Hoverflies

Adult

Characterized by their hovering, these flies are important predators of aphids. They lay eggs close to aphid colonies, and a single maggot can destroy about 800 aphids in its lifetime. They also help to control red spider mites on fruit trees, and lackey moth caterpillars.

Larva

Stiletto flies

Larva

Adult flies have long, tapering abdomens that resemble stilettos. They are predatory; adult flies conceal themselves among low plants or on the soil and prey upon other insects. The slender, predatory larvae resemble wireworms and live in the soil.

Other beneficial insects

Mites: Several mites are pests of gardens, orchards and greenhouse plants, but one of them, *Anystis agilis*, aggressively attacks other mites and insects, especially in orchards.
Brown lacewings: In addition to the green and powdery lacewings (see opposite page), brown lacewings help control aphids, thrips and mites.

RANGE OF OTHER BENEFICIAL CREATURES

• **Centipedes:** Distinguished from millipedes (which damage plants, have a sluggish nature and two pairs of short legs on most body segments) by having one pair of legs on each segment. Centipedes are active creatures and eat slugs, woodlice, mites, leatherjackets, grubs and other insects • **Frogs and toads:** These amphibians have a special liking for slugs and soon keep them under control. Both frogs and toads live in ponds, but are especially useful in a wildlife garden

• **Garden spiders:** These are varied but most spin webs that trap insects • **Hedgehogs:** Well-known animal with a voracious appetite for slugs, worms, beetles, earwigs, cutworms and millipedes. Do not disturb them in winter while they are hibernating; check bonfire sites for them before igniting rubbish. Do not provide them with saucers of bread soaked in milk, as this causes diarrhoea in youngsters • **Shrews** and **slow-worms** are also beneficial.

OTHER WAYS TO REDUCE PEST AND DISEASE PROBLEMS

Apart from encouraging plant-friendly insects and beneficial creatures into gardens, there are other things you can do:

• Keep the soil healthy by regularly adding decayed garden compost (pages 12–47) and digging in green manure crops (see pages 54–57).

• Rotate vegetable garden crops on a yearly basis (see right and page 46).

• Try companion planting (see below).

• Select cultivars (varieties) that are resistant to pests and diseases (see below).

CROP ROTATION

Growing vegetables continuously on the same piece of soil from one year to another encourages the build-up of pests and diseases. Also, where crops are not rotated the soil becomes depleted of certain plant foods.

Resistant plants

Cultivars of a few plant species have a degree of resistance to some pests and diseases. For example, some butterhead lettuces possess a resistance to lettuce root aphid, while some roses have a resistance to diseases such as black spot, rose rust and powdery mildew.

Companion planting

By using specific plants in association with each other, pest attacks can be diminished. For example:
• **Chives** planted between roses help to keep them free of aphids • **Garlic, leeks and onions** grown around beds of carrots help to cloak their distinctive aroma and to confuse carrot flies
• **Nasturtiums** especially entice aphids; therefore, plant French marigolds (*Tagetes patula*) nearby as they attract hoverflies that feed on aphids • **Spearmint** and **garlic** help to confuse and deter aphids.

Leafmould

What exactly is leafmould?

This consists of fallen leaves from deciduous shrubs and trees that have been collected and encouraged to decompose. The leaves can be added in limited amounts to compost heaps and bins, but are best put in a well-aerated enclosure to decay, which takes up to two years. The leafmould is then used as a mulch or dug into the soil. Apart from using fallen leaves for leafmould, raking up and composting them tidies up the garden.

CAN I USE LEAVES FROM EVERGREEN TREES AND SHRUBS?

These are much tougher than those of deciduous types, and throughout the year are best raked up as they fall from shrubs and trees and burned. The ash can be shallowly dug into the soil in autumn or winter. Do not use the foliage from conifers (whether evergreen or deciduous) to make leafmould, as they will take too long to rot down.

IS LEAFMOULD SUITABLE FOR ADDING TO SEED AND POTTING COMPOSTS?

Loam-based seed and potting composts are formed of partially sterilized loam to ensure that plant-damaging pests and diseases are not present. Therefore, to add leafmould to these compost mixtures is not sensible, as it would contaminate the compost and put plants at risk from pests and diseases.

COLLECTING FALLEN LEAVES

Wire-tined rakes are easy to use and ideal for removing leaves from lawns.

The task of collecting fallen leaves is influenced by the size of your garden. Here are a few ways to collect them.
- A traditional besom brush is ideal, as it can remove leaves from lawns as well as from gutters along their edges.
- Use a wire-tined rake on a lawn to remove fallen leaves. The tines are especially useful for clawing out leaves that have become trodden into a lawn's surface.
- To pick up leaves and to put them in a wheelbarrow, use two pieces of 12–18 mm (½–¾ in) thick wood, 23 cm (9 in) wide and 50 cm (20 in) long. Draw them together to lift up and remove the leaves (see page 5).
- Proprietary leaf carts aid the easy raking up and collecting of leaves, especially on a lawn.
- Wheeled or hand-held leaf-vacuum machines are available, and these are designed to suit both large and small gardens.

Powered leaf collectors are a good choice for clearing leaves from large lawns.

A besom (formed of twiggy sticks) is ideal for use on small lawns.

Hand-held leaf-vacuum machines soon clear dry leaves from lawns.

LEAF BINS

An enclosure for raked-up leaves is essential if they are not to be blown back over a garden. A wire-mesh bin, circular or square and 60–75 cm (2–2½ ft) across and 75–90 cm (2½–3 ft) high, is ideal. Position it in slight shade to prevent the leaves rapidly becoming dry. A wind-sheltered position is ideal to ensure the bin is not blown over during winter gales and the leaves rescattered over the garden. Regularly add water to the leaves in summer, and cover with a piece of old carpet in winter if the weather is exceptionally wet. Decomposition takes up to two years. Therefore, you will need two of these leaf bins to cope with a yearly cycle of fresh leaves that need to be turned into leafmould. Never mix one year's leaves with those from the following season, as they will be at a different stage of decomposition.

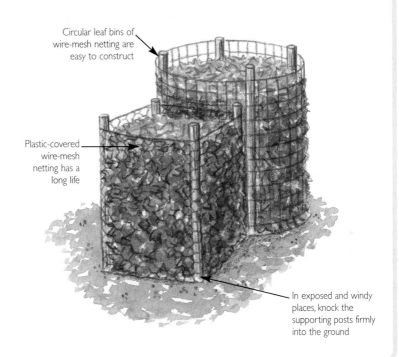

Circular leaf bins of wire-mesh netting are easy to construct

Plastic-covered wire-mesh netting has a long life

In exposed and windy places, knock the supporting posts firmly into the ground

Plastic sacks

In small gardens, a strong, polythene bag is an ideal way to store and convert the leaves into leafmould. Fill a bag with leaves, mix in lawn mowings and dampen the mixture with water. Then, pierce holes in the base and sides of the bag to enable air to enter and excess moisture to escape. Tie up the top and place the bag in an out-of-the-way position. After about a year, check if the leaves have decomposed. If not, resecure the top and leave for another few months. When fully decomposed, use as a mulch or dig into the soil.

CAN I SPEED UP THE DECOMPOSITION OF LEAVES IN LEAF BINS?

There are several ways to speed up this process:
• Mix lawn mowings with the leaves, but ensure they are not put in thick layers.
• Add garden soil in thin layers – it contains bacteria and soil organisms that encourage and speed up the decomposition process.
• Water the leaves during summer – moisture is essential for the decomposition process, but do not waterlog them so that air is excluded.
• In autumn and before raking leaves from a lawn, use a lawn mower to chop up the leaves to encourage them to decay quickly. Powered leaf collectors and shredders are available (see opposite).

HOW CAN I USE LEAFMOULD?

You can either use it in spring and early summer as a 7.5 cm (3 in) mulch around shrubs and herbaceous perennials, as well as between strawberry plants and rows of soft fruits, or dig it into the soil in autumn or winter to improve it. When using leafmould as a mulch, it should not touch the plants. Eventually, it will decompose and can be hoed into the soil.

Use leafmould to mulch between, but not touching, strawberry plants.

The composting process

Organic matter, from old cabbage leaves to teabags and annual garden weeds, decomposes in a heap or bin, creating a nutrient-rich material that can be dug into the soil or used as a mulch. This process is influenced by several environmental factors, ranging from the time of year to weather conditions. The method used to decompose the material also has an influence on the rate at which it is converted into compost for the garden.

Plastic-type compost bins are ideal for use in small gardens.

When will it be ready to use?

Garden compost, ready to be used

The time taken for organic material in a compost heap or bin to decay and be ready for use in gardens is influenced by the materials in it and the time of year. A compost heap started in spring or early summer will be ready for use in late autumn (or the following spring if begun in late summer); one created in autumn will have material ready during the following late summer or autumn. However, the main way to judge the readiness of the material for use is by its colour and smell (see 'When is composting complete?' opposite).

THE DECOMPOSITION PROCESS

In nature, the process of converting organic material into a decomposed material that can be used to enrich soil is a continuing cycle. It involves the activities of millions of bacteria and many different and often microscopic soil organisms, as well as more visible and recognizable creatures such as slugs and snails.

Many types of bacteria are present and these include psychrophiles, which begin the process of decomposition when temperatures are relatively low, at about 13°C (55°F). These are followed by mid-temperature bacteria, mesophiles, which live at temperatures of 20–30°C (68–86°F), then

thermophiles which function at temperatures of 40–70°C (104–158°F).

Other essential occupants include fungi, such as actinomycetes and streptomycetes, as well as nematodes that prey upon protozoa, fungal spores and bacteria. There are also mites, which feed on the yeasts in fermenting materials. Further creatures present at various stages in the decomposition process include red worms (also known as manure worms, red wigglers, tiger worms and brandlings; see pages 48–49), spiders, springtails, slugs and snails, centipedes and ground beetles.

ENVIRONMENTAL INFLUENCES

The speed at which organic material decomposes is influenced by several factors, in addition to the types of material in the compost heap.

- **Cold weather:** In cold weather, the composting process in a compost heap almost ceases, especially when newly created and when high-temperature bacteria have yet to operate. Compost heaps open to snow and cold rain are especially likely to suffer with temperature drops, as well as those in cold, windy and exposed positions.

Wooden compost bins (usually formed of three compartments) are ideal in large gardens and on allotments.

- **Hot weather:** Warmth encourages rapid decomposition, although very high temperatures cause the compost heap to dry rapidly. Therefore, it is best to cover the compost and water it regularly during hot summers to keep the materials lightly moist.
- **Light and shade:** The decomposing process in a compost heap also functions in darkness and therefore the only influence of darkness or light is on the temperature of the heap's ingredients.
- **Air:** This is essential to microbial life and activity in the compost heap. Ensure that air is present and that moisture is not filling all of the air spaces. This is achieved by creating layers of different types of material, as well as turning over the heap (see pages 38–39).
- **Wet weather:** The composting process requires moisture, but not total saturation. Covering a compost heap with a piece of old carpet prevents torrential rain causing problems by reducing the temperature and creating conditions unsuitable for bacteria and other compost organisms. In addition, an excessive amount of water will prevent air entering the compost heap, causing it to become anaerobic and the microbial life to die. It is usually recommended that the moisture content should be about 50 per cent, with a level below 40 per cent or over 60 per cent causing problems. In practice this can be difficult to judge, but an easy way to assess if the right level of moisture is being achieved is to slightly burrow into the heap – if creatures are actively present and the compost slightly moist, the level of moisture is about right. Another method is to squeeze a handful of compost – if a few drops of moisture escape, again the moisture content is about right.

Plastic compost bins are available in many shapes and sizes – you should avoid those that are too tall to be filled easily.

- **Dry weather:** This is also detrimental to bacteria and other occupants in a compost heap, causing their deaths or encouraging them to move elsewhere as the material starts to become radically dry. Covering with a lid or carpet helps to conserve moisture, but regularly check the moisture content and add water as necessary.
- **Soil on which the compost heap is formed:** Ensure that this soil is well drained and free from perennial weeds (see pages 26–27).

WHEN SHOULD I START COMPOSTING?

You can begin creating a compost heap at any time, although throughout summer and when clearing up flower borders and vegetable plots in autumn and early winter are the most popular times.

WHEN IS COMPOSTING COMPLETE?

When the compost is brown, crumbly, without any obnoxious smells and slightly warm or cool. The ingredients earlier added to the heap should not be identifiable. Take care not to use the compost too early, when there is still some microbial activity, since at that stage when mixed with soil it will use up nitrogen that is present and reduce its availability to plants.

TESTING FOR LAWN WEEDKILLERS

If you have moved to another garden, inherited a compost heap and are unsure if lawn weedkillers were applied to grass cuttings present in the heap, you must test it before use. Take a sample of material from the compost heap, mix it with peat-based potting compost and place in a seed-tray (flat). The test is to sow radish or cress seeds; if they germinate and the seedlings grow healthily, the material is fine to use.

What can I compost?

Is all food waste compostable?

Organic kitchen waste can be added to a compost heap, where it will slowly decompose and later be used as a mulch or for digging into the soil during autumn and winter. Some of the peelings and waste from fresh vegetables may be thick and tough, but eventually they will break down. You can also use leftover meals, but avoid strong-smelling meat and fish material as this can cause problems by attracting mice and rats.

KITCHEN WASTE TO ADD TO COMPOST HEAPS

A wire-netting and plastic-sheeting compost bin.

Each year, kitchens produce large amounts of vegetable waste and most of it can be put on a compost heap. Here are the main materials to consider.

Coffee grounds
They can be added to compost heaps or bins or mixed with earlier decomposed compost and either forked into the soil or used as a mulch. The nutritional value of coffee grounds varies, but expect up to 2 per cent nitrogen, less than 1 per cent phosphate and varying amounts of potash. Worms appear to find coffee grounds especially attractive.

Decaying fruits and vegetables
Fruits and vegetables that have decayed to the point where they are inedible can be added to compost heaps or bins.

However, in late summer decaying fruits especially will attract wasps, so remember to cover the heap if anyone is working in its vicinity.
Other garden uses: Old and decaying potatoes cut in half and placed outside near plants will lure earwigs; later, remove and destroy these pests. In addition, grapefruit skins put outside will entice slugs and snails, which also can be removed and destroyed each morning.

Eggshells
These are brittle and hard and do not decompose quickly, but they can be added to compost heaps; crush them first to encourage faster decay.
Other garden uses: Broken eggshells are ideal for sprinkling around plants in an attempt to prevent slugs and snails reaching the plants.

Rhubarb leaves
Although the leaves are poisonous to eat and are therefore cut off during the preparation of stalks (sometimes known as 'sticks') for cooking, they can be put on a compost heap.

Teabags
Adding teabags to a compost heap helps to make use of the 3,000 bags (often more) a family of four might use in a year. When wet, they retain large amounts of moisture and therefore are best spread evenly over the heap's surface, rather than in one area. They are rich in plant foods, containing as much as 4 per cent nitrogen and up to 1 per cent each of phosphate and potash.

Tea leaves
Similarly to teabags, tea leaves or grounds can be used; they contain about the same amount of plant foods as teabags.

Is wood ash suitable?

Wood-burning stoves each year produce masses of ash, and this can be added to a compost heap. It is rich in plant foods and contains 5–10 per cent potash, 35 per cent calcium and 1.5 per cent phosphate. When cold, sprinkle the ash fresh (without allowing it to get wet) on the heap, then cover immediately with a layer of other composting materials. If the ash is allowed to become wet, the potash will leach away. Do not use coal or coke ash in a compost heap, as these contain substances that are harmful to plants.

What should I do with food packaging?

Most packet foods are well packaged and many people wonder what to do with the coverings. Cellophane or plastic packaging must be put out for landfill, but paper or cardboard packaging can be added to a recycling bin or used in limited amounts, after being shredded, in wormeries (see pages 48–53) or compost heaps.

What should I do with aluminium foil?

If clean, it can be screwed up tightly and put into a recycling bin. If covered in the residues of fat or baked-on food, place in a landfill bin.

Other garden uses: Cut into strips, about 2.5–5 cm (1–2 in) wide, and attach to trees or bamboo canes to scare birds away from ripening fruits, sown seeds, young seedlings and plants. Do remember that, although birds can be frightened away, they must not be harmed (birds are legally protected in some countries).

Can I use hair?

Both human and animal hair can be added to a compost heap. Spread it evenly over the surface, rather than in one area, especially if there are large amounts of it. Thoroughly moisten it before adding to the heap to encourage decay, although this is never quick. Hair is rich in fertilizers, with about 3 kg (6½ lb) of hair containing as much nitrogen as 45–90 kg (100–200 lb) of manure.

Can I add wool?

In earlier years, farmers living close to woollen textile mills added wool waste (known as 'shoddy') to the soil. On a much smaller scale, wool and other natural-fibre fabrics can be used in a compost heap or bin. Break up the fabric into small pieces to enable rapid decomposition. These materials contain 3.5–6 per cent nitrogen, 2–4 per cent phosphate and 1–3.5 per cent potash. Do not use synthetic fabrics, as they will not decompose.

Composting garden waste

Can I compost all of my garden waste?

Most waste left over from growing food and ornamental crops in gardens, greenhouses, conservatories and on patios can be composted. Poultry and farmyard manure, spent mushroom compost, straw and even seaweed and sawdust are excellent candidates for a compost heap. Peat-based compost left in pots and tubs after summer-flowering plants have been removed can also be used. The compost in old growing-bags is another useful material that can be recycled.

VEGETABLE WASTE

'Vegetable waste' includes any soft-tissued material that was once alive. It should not be affected by persistent plant diseases, such as clubroot; if this is the case, it should always be burned rather than composted. Non-compostable materials are detailed on pages 20–21.

- **Annual, biennial and herbaceous plants** Add soft stems and/or whole plants to compost heaps and bins throughout the summer, and especially in the autumn when clearing up flower beds and herbaceous flower borders.

- **Annual and biennial weeds** These can be composted as they are pulled up throughout the summer, and in the autumn when tidying the garden ready for the winter; see pages 18–19 for descriptions and illustrations of suitable types.

- **Dead flowers** Throughout the summer, when cutting off dead flowers from border plants and those grown in containers on a patio, add them to a compost heap.

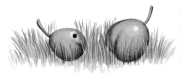

- **Fallen fruits** Apples and pears that fall prematurely from fruit trees are ideal for adding to a compost heap or bin. In addition, add those that had been stored but deteriorated before they could be eaten.

- **Fallen leaves** Deciduous trees shed their leaves in autumn. Add the leaves in small amounts to compost heaps, or make them into leafmould (see pages 10–11 for details of making leafmould and its uses).

- **Grass mowings** Throughout summer, add in thin layers to a compost heap; mix the mowings with fibrous waste to enable air to penetrate. Do not compost grass cuttings which have been cut from a lawn recently treated with a selective herbicide (weedkiller); these can soon damage plants.

- **Hedge clippings** Add clippings from deciduous, soft-textured hedging plants throughout the year. Those from evergreen shrubs are best shredded, as they do not decompose readily.

- **Prunings** Soft prunings can be added to compost heaps, but woody shoots are best shredded and used as a mulch.

- **Shredded bark** This takes a long time to decay in a compost heap, so it is better to use it as a mulch.

- **Unharvested vegetables** Includes root vegetables (carrots, turnips and parsnips), salad crops (lettuces, radishes and spring onions) and other vegetables (cabbages, Brussels sprouts and beans). To speed up their decay, cut up tough stems before adding them to a compost heap or bin.

What can't I compost?

There are many garden and household materials that cannot be added to compost heaps. These are described on pages 20–23. Advice about dealing with woody waste is given on pages 24–25.

OTHER GARDEN AND COUNTRY WASTE

Country and animal waste

These types of waste include a wide range of materials and sources, from pet bedding to farmyards and stables.

- **Farmyard manure** Add in small amounts to compost heaps; it is better dug into soil in autumn or winter, where it provides nutrients for plants and improves the soil.

- **Guinea pig and rabbit droppings and bedding** Mix in thin layers with other compost. These family pets are vegetarians and therefore their droppings, as well as their bedding (especially when straw), is ideal for adding to compost heaps.

- **Hay** Add in thin layers to a compost heap. Alternatively, use it as a mulch (where it will not be blown about) or dig into the soil in autumn and early winter (but later the soil may need an added dressing of nitrogen to replace that removed during decomposition).

- **Poultry manure** Chicken, duck, geese and pigeon manure can be added in thin layers to a compost heap or bin, where its richness in nitrogen makes it ideal for 'activating' the heap. It can be toxic if added directly to the soil.

- **Sawdust** Avoid thick layers, and check that it does not contain toxic chemicals. It is best to compost it before adding it to the soil, although it can be used to form a 2.5 cm (1 in) thick mulch that is later hoed into the soil surface. Unfortunately, it is likely to blow about in dry and windy weather, or become compacted during wet periods.

- **Seaweed** Wash off the salt and add in limited amounts to a compost heap. Preferably, dig into the soil in autumn or winter. Remember that permission may be required to remove it from beaches.

- **Spent hops** Usually bought in large amounts. Add in thin layers to compost heaps, but preferably dig it into sandy soils to assist moisture retention.

- **Spent mushroom compost** Usually alkaline in nature; use it in thin layers in a compost heap, but preferably dig it into soil (especially if the soil is acidic).

- **Stable manure and bedding** Horse, pony and donkey bedding and manure can be added in thin layers to compost heaps; preferably dig it into the soil in autumn or winter. It helps to improve the soil's structure, as well as adding nutrients.

- **Straw** Ideal for adding in layers to a compost heap. Alternatively, dig it into the soil in autumn and early winter (but later the soil may need an added dressing of nitrogen to replace that removed during decomposition).

Old potting compost

Inevitably, during each year plants growing indoors or in conservatories and greenhouses, are discarded through old age or their displaying coming to an end. Their rootballs, as well as unused potting and seed composts, can be recycled as described below.

- **Growing-bags** After one season, peat-based compost in growing-bags can be treated in several ways. It can be revitalized for the following season by topping up with peat and adding fertilizers, added in thin layers to compost heaps, mixed with the surface soil in borders, or used as a mulch.

- **Houseplant compost** Compost from dead plants can be broken up and added in limited amounts to compost heaps and bins. Alternatively, scatter it over border soil.

- **Patio container compost** Old and used compost from tubs, pots, hanging-baskets, windowboxes, wall-baskets and other containers can be broken up and added in small amounts to compost heaps. Alternatively, add to borders.

Composting weeds

Which weeds can I compost?

There are many annual garden weeds that can be added to a compost heap or bin throughout summer, when hoed up or just pulled out of flower beds and borders. Vegetable plots and herb gardens also need regular weeding and a compost heap is a convenient place to put these soft-textured and short-lived weeds. In autumn and early winter, when annuals naturally die, they can be composted, as can biennials.

ANNUAL WEEDS

The range of annual weeds in gardens and allotments is wide, and some are described here (suitable for composting).

- *Agrostemma githago* (**Corn Cockle**): Tall, with pale red-purple flowers.
- *Anthemis arvensis* (**Corn Chamomile**): Erect habit, with white and yellow daisy-like flowers.
- *Anthemis cotula* (**Stinking Mayweed; Stinking Chamomile**): Erect, with white flowers.

Anthemis cotula

- *Atriplex patula* (**Common Orache; Iron Root**): Much-branched, with triangular leaves and inconspicuous green flowers.
- *Capsella bursa-pastoris* (**Shepherd's Purse**): Sometimes a biennial; deeply lobed leaves and white flowers.
- *Chenopodium album* (**Fat Hen; Goosefoot**): Tall and erect, with white or pink flowers.
- *Chrysanthemum segetum* (**Corn Marigold**): Occasionally perennial; erect, with golden-yellow flowers.

Chenopodium album

- *Fumaria officinalis* (**Fumitory**): Weak and scrambling, with pink flowers.
- *Galium aparine* (**Cleavers; Goosegrass**): Straggling and clinging, with dull white flowers.
- *Hyoscyamus niger* (**Henbane**): Foetid and very poisonous; creamy-yellow flowers with purple veins.
- *Lapsana communis* (**Nipplewort**): Tall and branching, with yellow flowers.
- *Matricaria matricarioides* (**Rayless Mayweed; Wild Chamomile; Pineapple Weed**): Sometimes known as *M. chamomilla*; aromatic, with white and yellow flowers.
- *Papaver rhoeas* (**Field Poppy**): Tall and erect, with deep scarlet flowers, usually with dark centres.
- *Polygonum aviculare* (**Knotgrass**): Low and spreading, with pink or white flowers.
- *Polygonum convolvulus* (**Black Bindweed; Climbing Buckwheat**): Twining stems and bell-shaped, greenish-white flowers.
- *Polygonum lapathifolium* (**Pale Persicaria**): Branched and spreading, with stems that often root at their leaf-joints, and white or pink flowers.

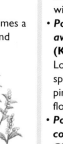
Papaver rhoeas

Polygonum persicaria

- *Polygonum persicaria* (**Redshank; Persicaria**): Sprawling, with white or pink flowers.
- *Senecio vulgaris* (**Groundsel**): Deeply lobed leaves and yellow flowers in loose clusters, often throughout the year.
- *Sherardia arvensis* (**Field Madder**): More or less prostrate, with pale-purple flowers.
- *Sinapis arvensis* (**Charlock; Wild Mustard**): Irregularly lobed leaves and yellow flowers.
- *Sisymbrium officinale* (**Hedge Mustard**): Tall and spreading stems and pale yellow flowers.
- *Solanum nigrum* (**Black Nightshade**): White and yellow flowers; poisonous berries.
- *Spergula arvensis* (**Corn Spurrey**): Sticky and hairy leaves, and white flowers.
- *Stellaria media* (**Chickweed**): Often prostrate, with white flowers.

Stellaria media

ANNUAL WEEDS (CONTINUED)

- *Urtica urens* (**Annual Nettle**): Nettle-like leaves and green flowers.
- *Veronica hederifolia* (**Ivy-leaved Speedwell**): Low and sprawling, with lobed, ivy-like leaves and purple-lilac to white flowers.

Urtica urens

- *Veronica persica* (**Common Field Speedwell; Buxbaum's Speedwell**): Branching, low and sprawling, with sky-blue flowers, sometimes throughout the year.
- *Viola arvensis* (**Field Pansy**): Low and short, with cream flowers, often tinted violet and yellow.

Removing annual weeds

Annual weeds can be pulled up, or hoed off close to the soil's surface by using a draw hoe or a Dutch hoe. Sharpening the cutting edge of these hoes makes it easier to sever annual weeds at ground level.

ANNUAL GRASSES

These grasses can be added to a compost heap and include the following:

- *Alopecurus myosuroides* (**Black Grass; Black Twitch; Slender Foxtail**): Loosely or compactly tufted, with green or purplish leaves and yellowish-green, pale green or purplish flowers.
- *Avena fatua* (**Wild Oat; Wild Oat Grass; Spring Wild Oat; Havers**): Tall and resembles cultivated oats, sometimes with reddish-brown flowers.

- *Avena ludoviciana* (**Winter Wild Oat; Wild Oat**): Stout annuals, similar to *A. fatua*.
- *Bromus mollis* (**Soft Brome; Lop Grass**): Can also be biennial; erect or spreading, with greyish-green leaves and greyish-green or purplish flowers.
- *Bromus sterilis* (**Barren Brome**): Can also be biennial; somewhat untidy and sprawling, with green or purplish flowers.

- *Poa annua* (**Annual Meadow Grass**): Sometimes a short-lived perennial; spreading, with purple or green flowers.

Poa annua

BIENNIAL WEEDS

These are plants that grow from seeds and complete their life cycle in two seasons. During the first year, their seeds germinate and plants establish themselves in the soil; in the second season, they produce flowers and seeds and then die. There are fewer biennial weeds than annual types, and they include the following (suitable for composting):

- *Arctium lappa* (**Burdock; Great/Greater Burdock**): Broad, heart-shaped leaves and large, thistle-like heads of purple flowers.

Arctium lappa

Conium maculatum

- *Conium maculatum* (**Hemlock**): Tall, foetid and poisonous, with purple-spotted stems, finely cut leaves and white flowers.
- *Digitalis purpurea* (**Foxglove**): Sometimes perennial; tall stems tightly clustered with pink-purple, bell-shaped flowers.

- *Echium plantagineum* (**Purple Viper's Bugloss**): Sometimes known as *E. lycopsis*; erect and resembling *E. vulgare*, with red flowers becoming purple-blue.
- *Echium vulgare* (**Viper's Bugloss**): Sometimes perennial; pink flowers turning vivid blue.

Echium vulgare

Dealing with household waste

Which bits of rubbish are non-compostable?

Some household waste cannot be placed on a compost heap – this includes plastic bags and bottles, metal cans, glass bottles and jam-jars. You should place such items in special recycling bins for collection by your local authority, or take them to your nearest recycling centre. Some non-compostable materials can be adapted for use when sowing seeds or growing plants in gardens; ideas for these are suggested below.

TYPES OF HOUSEHOLD WASTE AND WHAT TO DO WITH THEM

The range of household waste is wide and includes many different materials, from paper and card to plastic and glass. Here is a list of these materials and the ways to recycle or dispose of them, as well as how to adapt them for use in gardens.

Aerosols
These can be added to recycling bins. Incidentally, do not buy those that contain CFCs (chlorofluorocarbons), which damage the ozone layer in the stratosphere.

Aluminium foil
If clean, crumple up tightly and add to a recycling bin. For use in gardens, see pages 14–15.

Egg boxes
These can be added to recycling bins.
Garden uses: Ideal for use when sowing seeds. Cut off the lid (which can also be used) and fill with seed compost. Either put a single seed in each section, or sow two or three seeds in each unit and later thin to the strongest.

Glass jars and bottles
Whatever the colour of glass jars and bottles (such as white, green or brown) they can, after being rinsed, be added to a recycling bin. This glass recycling does not include milk bottles, drinking glasses or window and mirror glass. 'Pyrex' cooking dishes are also not suitable.
Garden uses: If you grow vegetables such as cucumbers from seeds, sow three seeds together on a small mound of fertile soil out of doors and cover with a wide jam-jar to encourage quicker germination. Later, thin them to the strongest seedling.

Junk mail and envelopes
Consign these (even envelopes with windows) to a recycling bin.

Medicines and pills
Unused medicines and pills should be returned to your pharmacist. Do not flush them down the toilet, as chemicals in them will pollute watercourses, rivers and the sea, and adversely affect wildlife. Sometimes, they have a detrimental hormonal influence on fish and mammals.

Metal cans
Rinse and squash metal food and drink cans and put in a recycling bin. Recycling aluminium cans is especially environmentally friendly because the

Old and clean cans can be easily converted into string dispensers.

The tops and bottoms of egg boxes make ideal seed-trays (flats).

TYPES OF HOUSEHOLD WASTE (CONTINUED)

process uses 95 per cent less energy than when making them from new, and it results in less pollution.

Garden uses: You can make a string dispenser by drilling or punching a 6 mm (¼ in) hole in the base of a clean can (with its top cleanly removed). Push the end of the string through the hole and pop the ball of string inside. In addition, by making two holes on the top edge and attaching a string handle, you can hang it up.

Nappies (diapers)

Wrap securely in plastic bags and place in a general bin.

Paint tins

Take along to a recycling depot. Do not just add to a recycling bin.

Paper and card

Newspapers, magazines and card can be put in recycling bins; if soiled with food or other waste, place in a black bag for landfill.

Garden uses: Small amounts of shredded or crunched-up newspapers, together with paper kitchen towels, can be added to compost heaps. Moderate amounts of newspaper can be put into wormeries (see pages 48–53).

Plastic bottles

These should be washed and, if possible, squashed and placed in a recycling bin.

Garden uses: Cut the bases off large ones earlier used for milk and use them in the same way as glass jam-jars to encourage the early germination and development of seedlings. You can also cut off the base of a tall, tubular, plastic bottle (the type that washing-up liquid is sometimes sold in) and use it as a funnel to direct fuel into a petrol tank in a lawn mower.

Plastic packaging, wrapping, cartons and food trays

These are best placed in black bags for landfill.

Garden uses: Items that are firm and durable can be used as seed-trays (flats).

Polystyrene

Candidate for black bags and landfill.

Garden uses: Items that are rigid and deep can be used as seed-trays (flats).

Telephone directories

Place in a recycling bin.

'Tetra paks' (juice and milk cartons)

These are formed of recyclable materials and in some places may be added to a recycling bin (but check if this is true in your area).

CAN IT BE RECYCLED?

Because the type of material accepted by local authorities for recycling varies from one area to another, the suggestions here are only a guide and may, as recycling techniques improve, be changed.

You can create mini-greenhouses by inverting glass jars over plant pots.

All kinds of old pots and containers can be used for growing plants.

Dealing with perennial weeds

Which weeds cannot be composted?

Weeds that are 'perennial' – meaning they live for 2–3 years or more – should not be added to a compost heap because the temperatures reached during the composting process will not kill their roots. Later, when the compost is used in the garden, even the smallest part of a perennial weed's root system will regrow. It is best to burn them or put them in a plastic bag to decompose (see below).

Digging up perennial weeds

Unlike annual weeds, which can be pulled up or hoed off, perennial types must be carefully dug up to ensure that all of the roots are removed. Some perennial weeds are especially pernicious, and these include *Aegopodium podagraria* (Ground Elder), *Agropyron repens* (Couch Grass) and *Equisetum* spp. (Horsetails). When digging down into the soil to remove all of their roots, use a garden fork, rather than a spade, which would chop up the roots and make the problem even worse.

What should I do with perennial weeds?

Preferably you should burn them, but having a bonfire in a small garden may be impossible. In addition, garden fires cannot be lit in a smoke-free area. Therefore, put the roots in the green-waste recycling bins provided by some local authorities, or take them to a green-waste collection point.

Plastic bags

If there is no other way to get rid of perennial weeds, put them in a thick plastic bag that can be securely sealed. Then place them in an out-of-the-way position, where they will slowly decompose.

PERENNIAL WEEDS

A wide range of perennial weeds is to be found in gardens; some are described below.

- **Achillea millefolium (Yarrow; Milfoil):** Feathery, dark green leaves and white, pink and creamy flowers.
- **Achillea ptarmica (Sneezewort):** Stem-clasping leaves and creamy flowers.
- **Aegopodium podagraria (Ground Elder; Goutweed; Bishop's Weed; Herb Gerard):** Creeping and patch-forming, with white flowers.

Aegopodium podagraria

- **Atropa bella-donna (Deadly Nightshade; Dwale):** Tall, with well-branched stems and dull purple or greenish flowers; extremely poisonous.
- **Calystegia sepium (Bindweed; Large Bindweed; Bellbine):** Creeping or climbing, with arrow-shaped leaves and white, occasionally pink, flowers.

Calystegia sepium

- **Cardamine pratensis (Lady's Smock; Cuckoo Flower):** Tufted, with lilac or white flowers.

- **Centaurea montana (Perennial Cornflower):** Creeping habit, especially in grassy areas, with large, highly attractive, blue flowers.
- **Centaurea nigra (Black Knapweed; Lesser Knapweed; Hardhead):** Stout stem and blackish-brown and reddish-purple flowers.
- **Centaurea scabiosa (Knapweed; Greater Knapweed):** Branching stems and red-purple, thistle-like flowerheads.
- **Cichorium intybus (Chicory; Wild Succory):** Erect stems, deep tap root and bright blue flowers.
- **Cirsium acaule (Dwarf Thistle; Stemless Thistle):** Low, short and creeping, with red-purple flowerheads.
- **Cirsium arvense (Creeping Thistle):** Far-creeping, slender tap root, and lilac flowerheads.
- **Cirsium vulgare (Spear Thistle):** Sharply spined leaves and thistle-like heads with red-purple flowers.

PERENNIAL WEEDS (CONTINUED)

- *Equisetum arvense* (**Horsetail; Common Horsetail**): Pernicious, with creeping roots and upright stems resembling a horse's tail; many related species.

Equisetum arvense

- *Glechoma hederacea* (**Ground Ivy**): Low, creeping and with blue-purple flowers.
- *Lamium album* (**White Dead Nettle**): Creeping, with heart-shaped leaves and white flowers.
- *Leucanthemum vulgare* (**Ox-eye Daisy; Moon Daisy**): Sometimes known as *Chrysanthemum leucanthemum*, with daisy-like white and yellow flowers.
- *Linaria vulgaris* (**Common Toadflax; Toadflax; Yellow Toadflax**): Erect stems with yellow flowers.
- *Lychnis flos-cuculi* (**Ragged Robin**): Slender and branching, with bright pink flowers.

- *Petasites hybridus* (**Butterbur**): Low and patch-forming, with large, heart-shaped leaves and lilac-pink flowers.

Petasites hybridus

- *Pimpinella saxifraga* (**Burnet; Burnet Salad; Burnet Saxifrage**): Upright and slender, with white flowers.
- *Potentilla anserina* (**Silverweed**): Creeping, with long runners and silvery undersides on leaves; yellow flowers.
- *Prunella vulgaris* (**Self-heal**): Low and creeping, with violet flowers, occasionally pink or white.
- *Ranunculus bulbosus* (**Bulbous Buttercup**): Short, with a swollen base, deeply lobed leaves and golden-yellow flowers.
- *Ranunculus ficaria* (**Lesser Celandine**): Low and spreading, with dark green, heart-shaped leaves and yellow flowers.

Ranunculus ficaria

- *Ranunculus repens* (**Creeping Buttercup**): Creeping, with rooting runners, and yellow flowers.
- *Rumex obtusifolius* (**Broad-leaved Dock**): Erect and branched, with heart-shaped lower leaves and green flowers, sometimes turning red.

Ranunculus repens

- *Silene vulgaris* (**Bladder Campion**): Branching and woody base, and white flowers.
- *Solanum dulcamara* (**Bittersweet; Woody Nightshade**): Clambering or prostrate, with bright purple flowers in loose clusters.
- *Sonchus arvensis* (**Sow Thistle; Perennial Sow Thistle**): Tall and patch-forming, with rich yellow flowers.
- *Taraxacum officinale* (**Dandelion; Common Dandelion**): Leaves distinctly lobed, and characteristic yellow flowers.
- *Tussilago farfara* (**Coltsfoot**): Low, with a creeping rootstock and heart-shaped leaves, and yellow flowers.
- *Urtica dioica* (**Greater Stinging Nettle**): Large, nettle-like leaves and small green flowers.

PERENNIAL GRASSES

There are many of these grasses and, although some are attractive, others are pernicious and very difficult to eradicate. They include:

- *Agropyron repens* (**Couch Grass; Scutch; Twitch**): Far-spreading, with a creeping rootstock that often forms a dense mat.

Agropyron repens

- *Agrostis stolonifera* (**Creeping Bent Grass**): Tufted and spreading, with green, greyish-green or bluish-green leaves.
- *Briza media* (**Quaking Grass; Totter Grass; Doddering Dillies**): Creeping rootstock, with stem-clasping green leaves.
- *Holcus lanatus* (**Yorkshire Fog; Soft Creeping Grass**): Compact and tufted, with greyish-green or green leaves.

Briza media

Dealing with woody waste

What is woody waste?

Soft-leaved and young hedge clippings, such as those from regularly trimmed privet hedges, are ideal for composting when chopped into 7.5–10 cm (3–4 in) long pieces. However, tough wood left over from pruning shrubs and trees needs to be shredded into smaller pieces. These can be added in limited amounts (and in thin layers) to compost heaps, but are better used in spring and summer as a mulch on flower beds and around shrubs.

CHOOSING A SHREDDER

Safety is of the utmost importance when using a shredder (see opposite page, bottom right, for details).

Electric shredders are ideal for small gardens.

Innovative electric shredder with a collection box beneath.

There are shredders – in size and power source – to suit all home garden needs. Each type has its advantages and disadvantages:

- **Electric:** Wide range of sizes and prices, and able to shred wood up to 4 cm (1¾ in) thick. Long, outdoor power cables are usually needed, together with waterproof plugs and sockets if cables are joined.
- **Petrol-driven:** Many models to choose from, with some able to shred wood 7.5 cm (3 in) thick. A lockable garden shed (as far away as possible from your house) is essential for storing petrol in screw-top petrol cans. Do not use old plastic milk bottles.

Petrol-driven shredders can tackle thick stems.

HIRING OR BUYING?

The economics of buying or hiring a shredder, or engaging a shredding service, depend on several factors.

- If the amount of shredding is little and irregular, it is better to hire a shredder, but ask for confirmation from the hiring-out company that it is mechanically and electrically safe to use. In addition, check that you have transport for collecting and returning it.
- When buying, select the largest machine you can afford, as it will be more efficient than a small one and less likely to clog. It will also be able to tackle thicker material. Check that you are able to store it throughout the year in a dry, well-ventilated shed with a firm base.
- In some areas, shredding services are available from private contractors; this is ideal if you are not fully active and have only a small amount of shredding.

ARE SHREDDERS NOISY?

By their nature and the job they have to do, shredders are noisy, but some are noisier than others! Much depends on the shredder's size and if it is powered by electricity or petrol.

- Petrol-driven types are noisier than electric models and, although having the advantage of mobility, the constant running of the engine can cause neighbours to protest.
- Electric types are quieter when the engine is not 'in work', but noisy when shredding.
- The size and power of the shredder also influences the noise and a small machine when shredding thick branches can be noisier than a large one tackling the same-sized wood.
- Some electric shredders are marketed as 'quiet' types and this is certainly a bonus in town gardens.

HOW CAN I USE THE SHREDDINGS?

The shreddings can be used in several different ways.

- Add in small amounts to a compost heap. They can be encouraged to decompose more rapidly by first mixing them with grass mowings and by watering with a nettle liquid. This is formed from squashed nettles

PREPARING TO SHRED

Before starting to shred wood:
- Place all of the wood in one place, with the main stems towards you. This will make feeding the shredder quicker and easier. It is also an advantage to put the wood on the left side of the shredder (as you face it), if you are right-handed; it makes feeding the material into the machine easier.
- Put a container or wheelbarrow in place where it can collect shreddings direct from the machine.
- Until you feel confident in using the shredder, have a companion with you in case something goes wrong and the machine needs to be turned off quickly.
- Ensure that all safety checks have been made (see below right).

Always shred wood in a systematic way

placed in a bucket and with water added; leave for 2–3 weeks before use. In addition, diluted urine speeds up the composting process.
- Use immediately (and without composting) as a mulch around flowers and in shrub borders. Form a layer about 5 cm (2 in) thick. Unfortunately, birds disturb the shreddings in search of grubs in the damp soil beneath and may scatter the chippings over lawn edges.
- The shreddings can be put into a sealed black refuse bag. Eventually they will turn into compost if water is added and the bag is peppered with holes to allow air to enter. Decomposition usually takes 6–9 months, depending on the thickness of the chippings.

Use the chippings to form mulches around plants in shrub and flower borders.

CAN THE SHREDDINGS BE STORED?

Although chippings can be stored in a dry place, it is best to use them immediately (see left and above for their uses).

Safety when using a shredder

As with all garden equipment, care must be taken when using a shredder:

- When using an electric shredder, ensure that the cables are correct for outdoor use and that an electrical circuit breaker (sometimes known as a power breaker or residual current device) is installed in the wiring system.

- Do not wear loose and floppy clothing, especially ties and scarves.

- Wear stout boots, so that there is less risk of slipping and falling against the shredder.

- Wear protective glasses and a pair of strong gloves.

- Read the instructions before using the shredder and do not take any risks.

Siting the compost heap

**Where should
I put my
compost
heap?**

The best position is away from your house, near to the main source of plants that are to be composted and to where the finished compost will be chiefly used. The compost heap also needs to be out of direct view from ornamental areas and your house, although some compost-making enthusiasts like to make a feature of it. Easy accessibility throughout the year is also important, especially for gardeners who are impaired physically.

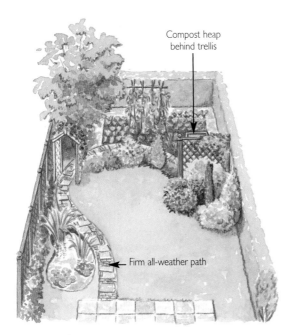

Compost heap
behind trellis

Firm all-weather path

A level site allows easy access to a compost heap or bin; make sure that paths are constructed from all-weather materials.

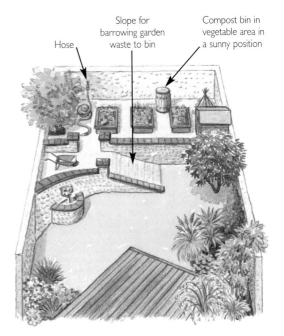

Slope for
barrowing garden
waste to bin

Compost bin in
vegetable area in
a sunny position

Hose

A sloping site makes it necessary to install a ramp to enable you to reach the compost heap or bin easily.

GETTING THE POSITION RIGHT

Before deciding on the compost heap's position, consider the following.

- **Aesthetic considerations:** Most gardeners do not wish for their compost heap to be on direct view from the house and therefore site it discreetly behind a hedge or ornamental trellis.
- **Well-drained soil:** Compacted soil does not readily absorb moisture and will cause run-off of excess water from torrential storms or if the compost heap is radically watered during dry weather. Therefore, before creating a compost heap, fork over the soil to a depth of 20–30 cm (8–12 in). It is also an opportunity to level the area, which will make the construction of compost heaps much easier than when on a slope.
- **Weed-free soil:** Before constructing a compost heap, check that the soil is not contaminated with perennial weeds (see pages 22–23). If present, there is a risk of them growing up

and into the compost and contaminating it with pernicious weeds that are difficult to eradicate.

- **Close to the vegetable garden:** The main source of material to be composted will be from a vegetable-growing area or a lawn. Therefore, a position close to them both is ideal, especially as most of the composted material is likely to be returned to these areas in autumn and winter.
- **Screening from strong wind:** To ensure that materials in the compost heap do not become dry, preferably position it in the shelter of a hedge sited on the side of the prevailing wind. This will, of course, help to screen it, but leave a space of 1.5–1.8 m (5–6 ft) between the hedge and the compost heap as the roots of the hedge spread widely and impoverish the soil of moisture.
- **Close to a water source:** During dry weather, a water source is useful, especially one that can be linked up to a hosepipe.

- **Not close to a wooden fence or garden shed:** Preferably, position a compost heap with a 1.2–1.5 m (4–5 ft) gap around it to enable it to be easily filled and emptied. Do not position one side next to a wooden fence or garden shed, as the compost will cause the wood to decay.
- **Warmth and sunshine:** A warm, sunny position initiates rapid decay in the compost heap. It will, however, also encourage drying; but this can be counteracted by covering it and regularly watering the heap in summer.
- **Not under a large tree:** Avoid positions under large, deciduous trees, because when they shed their foliage in autumn the leaves could contaminate fully decomposed compost currently being used. The leaves contain high amounts of carbon and if allowed to mix with partly decayed compost will slow down its decomposition. If it is not possible to position the compost heap elsewhere, cover it in autumn and regularly rake up the fallen leaves and use them to make leafmould (see pages 10–11).

- **Screening and hedging:** In vegetable gardens, runner beans clambering over a row of bean poles or along string netting attached to supports at either end will create a colourful and practical screen. Tripods of bean poles are also useful for camouflaging a compost heap. Alternatively, at the end of a lawn or ornamental area erect a free-standing trellis and use it for annual climbers, such as *Lathyrus odoratus* (Sweet Pea), or more permanent types such as clematis or *Lonicera* spp. (Honeysuckle). If the trellis is exposed and at risk from breaking when repeatedly battered by winter winds, choose *Humulus lupulus* 'Aureus' (Yellow-leaved Hop). It is a herbaceous climber and therefore will be bare of leaves during blustery winter weather.
- **Firm, all-weather paths:** These are useful throughout the year, especially in autumn and winter when the garden is being cleared up and materials from the compost heap are moved to a vegetable plot, ready for digging into the soil.

CONSTRUCTING A TRELLIS TO SCREEN THE COMPOST HEAP

Free-standing trellises need sound construction, with posts well secured in concrete. The depth of the hole depends on the height of the screen (see below). In windy and exposed areas, and especially when the trellis is clad in evergreen climbers, increase the depths of the holes and lengths of the posts.

1 Dig a hole to the required depth (see below), plus 15 cm (6 in). Put clean rubble in the base.

2 Put the post in the hole and check that it is upright. Use a builder's spirit-level (carpenter's level). Knock a stake into the soil at an angle of 45°, ready for securing the post temporarily.

3 Use a long nail to secure the stake to the post (two stakes may be needed). Check again that the post is vertical.

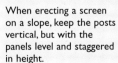
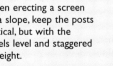
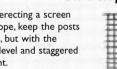

4 Use concrete to secure the post in position; then use a trowel to slope the concrete's surface away from the post. The trellis panels can now be firmly fixed to the posts.

DEPTHS OF HOLES AND HEIGHTS OF POSTS

- **Post 1.2 m (4 ft) above ground:** needs a post 1.6 m (5½ ft) long, in a hole 45 cm (1½ ft) deep.
- **Post 1.5 m (5 ft) above ground:** needs a post 2.1 m (7 ft) long, in a hole 60 cm (2 ft) deep.
- **Post 1.8 m (6 ft) above ground:** needs a post 2.4 m (8 ft) long, in a hole 60 cm (2 ft) deep.

On a slope

When erecting a screen on a slope, keep the posts vertical, but with the panels level and staggered in height.

Compost heaps and bins

Which is the better method?

In nature, plants die and fall on the soil beneath them. Stems, leaves, flowers and fruits decay and are eventually drawn into the soil by the soil-improving activities of worms and other soil creatures. In a garden or allotment, this decomposing process needs to be organized and a compost heap or bin provides a neat and tidy place for this to happen. As an alternative to compost heaps and bins, trenches and holes are a possibility (see page 29).

COMPOST HEAP OR COMPOST BIN?

Although these perform the same role in a garden, they are slightly different.
- A traditional compost heap, usually 1.2–1.5 m (4–5 ft) wide and high, and 1.8 m (6 ft) or more long, is formed of layers of waste organic material. It is not enclosed along its sides, but often covered to prevent the contents becoming dry or too wet. A cover also helps to retain warmth in the heap, especially in winter.
- Compost bins differ from heaps in that they retain the organic material in an often fully enclosed area. They are ideal for keeping the garden tidy and are usually made of wood or plastic. In addition, there are hybrid types, where medleys of materials, including breeze-blocks, wire-netting and wood, are used (see pages 36–37).
Proprietary types, either wood or plastic, are widely available and are perfect for use in most home gardens (see pages 32–33). There is also a compost tumbler (see page 33) that creates compost slightly more quickly.

Traditional compost heap made of layers of organic material

Compost bins provide a tidy way to create compost

Plastic compost bins are ideal for small gardens

INFLUENCE OF THE WEATHER

The time of year and the weather have a radical influence on the speed at which compost decomposes. Composting organisms and creatures are more active in warm weather than during cold periods. Here are a few ways to overcome the problems of excessive cold or warmth.

In cold climates
- Keep compost heaps covered with a thick carpet or black polythene (it retains more warmth than clear sheeting).
- Use an insulative jacket in winter on a compost bin to keep the compost warm. Proprietary covers are available; alternatively, encapsulate within a piece of thick carpet.
- Positioning the compost bin under trees (but not large, deciduous ones) gives some protection from frost and low

temperatures when there is little cloud cover in winter.
- Positioning a compost heap or bin in the shelter of a hedge helps to prevent cold winds cooling it.

In hot climates
- Regularly check that the compost heap is not becoming dry; if necessary, thoroughly drench it with water. Then cover it to prevent the material becoming dry again.
- Material in a compost bin is less at risk from becoming dry than in a compost heap.
- In hot climates, compost trenches and holes (see page 29) have many advantages, but ensure that torrential rain does not make the material too wet; air is excluded and aerobic decomposition is prevented.

Compost trenches and holes

As an alternative to heaps and bins, organic waste from kitchens and gardens can be composted in trenches or holes. This is an especially popular way to decompose waste material in late summer and autumn, when there are usually large amounts of organic waste from vegetable plots as well as the rest of the garden to be composted. It also saves on space for a compost heap or the cost of buying a compost bin.

What are compost trenches and holes?

COMPOST TRENCH

If having a compost heap or bin is an impossibility, try burying organic waste in a trench (the waste is left there to improve the soil). This system of decomposing waste is especially suitable in late summer and autumn. The speed at which the organic waste decomposes depends on the nature of the soil; if light, sandy and well aerated, decomposition is quicker than if in clay soil.

Organic material left to decompose in a trench usually partly depletes the soil of nitrogen. Therefore, be prepared to add an extra application of a nitrogenous fertilizer to the soil during the following early summer, when young plants are planted over the trench. Runner beans, French beans and courgettes are ideal vegetables to choose for these areas.

1 *Dig a trench, 38–45 cm (15–18 in) deep and wide, across a vegetable plot (keeping the topsoil separate). Ensure that perennial weeds (see pages 22–23) are not dug up and left in the trench. Instead, remove and burn them or place them in a sealed plastic bag.*

2 *Fill the trench with vegetable waste to within 15 cm (6 in) of the surface. Thoroughly water the material and tread it flat. Add further material, again to 15 cm (6 in) below the surface, then water and tread flat.*

3 *Replace all the soil (leaving the topsoil to last). Initially, the area over the trench will form a continuous mound, but by late spring it will have settled and this is an indication that the material has decomposed and the trench is ready for planting.*

Alternatively, fill the trench in small stages (as and when waste organic material is available). However, always cover the waste material with soil so that is not scattered over the garden, or becomes attractive to rodents. Draw back the covering of soil when further organic waste is added. Then, re-cover.

Compost holes

This is a variation on compost trenches and is ideal for small gardens, or when growing only a few vegetables. In autumn, dig a hole that is 38–45 cm (15–18 in) deep and 45–60 cm (18–24 in) square, and fill it with organic waste to within 15 cm (6 in) of the soil's surface. Tread down the waste and thoroughly water. Again fill, water and tread down. Then replace the soil. In spring, erect a wigwam of bean poles over the area and sow or plant runner beans to clamber over them.

Quick composting

This is a good way to speed up the decomposition of garden waste by enabling an increased amount of air to penetrate the mixture. Normally, material in a compost heap started in spring or early summer will be ready for use in late autumn (or the following spring if only begun in late summer), while one created in autumn will have material ready during the following late summer or autumn. However, quick composting speeds this up.

HOW CAN I UNDERTAKE QUICK COMPOSTING?

There are two ways to encourage organic waste from gardens and kitchens to decompose rapidly. Both of these methods utilize the fact that vegetable waste decomposes more rapidly if air is regularly mixed with it.

- Use a compost tumbler – a plastic bin that can be rotated (see opposite) to introduce air to the mixture. Remember to rotate it regularly.
- Completely fill a relatively low compost bin all at once, rather than adding material over several weeks or months. Fork over and turn the material several times a week.

Garden compost is invaluable, so the faster you can make it the better.

MAKING QUICK COMPOST

It is best to do this in late summer or very early autumn, when there is often a mass of garden waste available for composting. This material ranges from summer-flowering bedding plants and old herbaceous perennials to grass cuttings, soft hedge clippings and waste material from a vegetable plot.

1 *Gather into one place a large amount of garden waste and chop up thick stems into small pieces. Mix all parts of it together and add manure from horses and waste material from family pets, such as guinea pigs and rabbits.*

2 *Dig over a piece of ground (free from perennial weeds) and place on it the bottom part of a wood-framed compost bin, about 1.2 m (4 ft) square and formed of individual stackable sides, each 15–20 cm (6–8 in) deep.*

3 *When the ingredients are well mixed, place inside the base unit to a depth of 15–20 cm (6–8 in) and firmly tread over them. Then thoroughly water, especially at the edges where the mixture first becomes dry.*

MAKING QUICK COMPOST (CONTINUED)

4 *Add a further stackable side and fill with a further medley of the compostable material. Again, firm the layer and add water. Proceed like this until 3–4 levels have been created.*

5 *To keep the material moist and to help retain warmth in the heap, cover with a thick piece of carpet. Alternatively, use a sheet of black polythene. These coverings also help to prevent cold rain cooling the heap.*

6 *At least twice a week, remove the covering and use a garden fork to completely turn over and mix up the ingredients. If the material becomes dry, add water; if too wet, add further material to absorb excess moisture.*

7 *When the material is brown and crumbly, and without any obnoxious smells, it is ready to be used in a garden. It can be slightly warm or cool, and the ingredients should not be identifiable.*

USING A COMPOST TUMBLER

These tumblers are best used in summer, when the temperature is high and more conducive to rapid composting than in winter.
- Collect the waste material together and break up thick stems into thin pieces.

Compost tumblers are ideal in small gardens, where space is too limited for a traditional compost heap.

- Fill the tumbler (preferably at one single filling) about two-thirds full with vegetable waste from kitchens and gardens. Where possible, add horse manure or droppings from herbivorous (vegetarian) family pets, such as rabbits and guinea pigs.
- If the material is dry, add water, then secure the lid in place.
- Rotate the tumbler daily to enable air to mix with the waste material. Tumblers that rotate end-over-end are often difficult to tip over, especially if left untumbled for several days with compost settled at the base. However, regular rotation is essential.
- Every week, check that the material is moist.
- After about four weeks, see if the compost is ready to be used. Essentially, do not be guided by the time but by the nature of the compost inside the tumbler.

Can I use kitchen waste as well as garden waste?

You can use all vegetable waste from a kitchen, such as vegetable peelings and scraps. However, large amounts of leftover foods, and especially those containing meat and fish, are best put in a traditional compost heap.

Shop-bought compost bins

Is a proprietary bin essential?

Y ou can make your own bin (see pages 34–35), or even be really thrifty and use abandoned materials (see pages 36–37). For those with less time, shop-bought compost bins come in a range of sizes and shapes, some resembling plastic water-butts. Most plastic types are static, once positioned, while others have a tumbler facility (see below and page 31). Other proprietary bins are made of wood and arrive in a 'flat pack' of pieces.

Plastic compost bins can be quickly and easily positioned close to the source of organic waste.

WHAT SIZE DO I NEED?

Buy a plastic-type composting bin to suit the volume of material your garden and kitchen generates within a six-month period. Remember that you may eventually need three compost bins, so that the cycle of filling, decomposing and emptying proceeds systematically. The bins start at a capacity of about 220 litres (58 gallons) and go up to 330 litres (87 gallons) and these are ideal for most home gardeners; for larger areas, ones of 750 litres (198 gallons) are available. The larger the bin, the less it is influenced by cool temperatures in winter. Small ones cool rapidly and are best given a thermal winter jacket.

IS A PLASTIC TYPE BETTER THAN WOOD?

- A plastic bin looks neat and the outside can easily be kept clean while it is being filled with kitchen and garden organic waste. In addition, when emptied the inside can be scrubbed clean and thoroughly rinsed with water from a hosepipe.

- Plastic has fewer insulative qualities than wood. This is especially important for a small plastic compost bin, as low winter temperatures inhibit rapid decomposition. However, insulative jackets are available for some of them.
- Plastic bins are easier than wooden compost bins to move when empty and after they complete each composting cycle.
- Easy-fitting lids are available to prevent excessive rain reaching the compost, making it too wet as well as lowering the compost's temperature.
- A range of sizes is readily available, to suit small as well as large gardens (see opposite).
- Some plastic compost bins are tumblers and so can be rotated, enabling air to readily mix readily with the compost and reduce the composting time.
- Plastic does eventually become brittle though and is likely to crack during low winter temperatures.

DOES THE COLOUR MATTER?

Black tends to be the best colour as it helps to keep the compost warm in winter. In addition, a black bin is usually less noticeable than a green or grey one and harmonizes well with the garden.

WOODEN COMPOST BINS

Wood has a natural appearance which helps it to blend in with the rest of the garden. The wood is usually treated with plant- and bug-friendly preservatives and, together with its insulative qualities, is an ideal compost holder. Moveable wood panels at the front enable easy filling and emptying. Check if there is a cover, although if there is none it is not disastrous since you can use a piece of thick, old carpet or thick, strong polythene instead.

Some wooden compost bins are modular; to ensure continuity of composting, there are three separate modules – one being filled, the second full of decomposing garden and kitchen organic materials, and the third having completed its process and ready to be emptied.

GETTING THE HEIGHT RIGHT

The usual height of a compost bin is 1.2 m (4 ft) but for many people this makes it too high for easy filling and emptying. If this happens, you can make a raised stepping area with a few breeze-blocks positioned at the base of the bin. This will make it easier to fill and empty. For safety, make the platform wide and firm.

QUICK GUIDE TO ASSESSING A PLASTIC COMPOST BIN

- Size to suit your garden (see page 32).
- Open at its base for standing directly on the soil. This enables organisms and creatures in the soil to enter the compost heap to initiate and assist in the decomposition process.
- Large opening at the top to enable easy filling and emptying (some also have a shutter at the base to allow easy emptying).
- Secure lid.
- Rigid and strong construction.
- Where possible, made from recycled plastic. Check with the manufacturer before buying.
- Because the tumbler type is fully exposed to the weather, it especially benefits from a thermal jacket.

A securely fitting lid is an essential part of a plastic compost bin.

Circular (raised or inset) ridges on a compost bin provide increased rigidity.

A trapdoor at the base enables easy removal of decomposed material.

Wide-based plastic compost bins are especially suitable for wind-exposed areas.

Big trapdoors are essential in very large plastic compost bins.

DUSTBIN CONVERSIONS

An old, large, plastic dustbin can be adapted to become a compost bin by drilling some holes in the base and then using a hacksaw to cut it out (slightly in from the edge, so that the bin's structural rigidity is maintained). In addition, drill 6–8 holes, each 18–25 mm (¾–1 in) wide, in the sides to enable air to enter. Retain the lid.

Compost tumbler

This is an innovation on a static plastic compost bin. A plastic barrel, usually with a capacity of 200 litres (about 52 gallons), is mounted on a steel frame which enables it to be rotated. By turning the plastic tumbler over 2–3 times a week, the compost separates and air is allowed to mix with it. This allows it quickly to reach high temperatures, enabling even grass cuttings, which often form a mat impermeable to air, to rapidly decompose in the increased oxygen. During summer, when the weather is warm, the decomposing process can be completed in four weeks; in cold weather this will be much longer (see page 31).

Home-made compost bins

Providing you have the ability to use a saw, and to nail or screw pieces of timber together, you can make your own compost bin. The timbers must be cut to precise measurements and with square ends, however, to allow you to assemble the compost bin easily. To facilitate construction, ensure that the well-drained soil beneath the bin is level in all directions. You should always use galvanized nails or rust-proof screws to hold the timbers together.

Home-made compost bins are just as functional as store-bought types, and can be made from recycled materials.

Corrugated-iron sheets, or wire-netting and metal posts, can also be used to form a functional compost area.

GETTING THE SIZE RIGHT

Opinions vary about the best size for a compost bin to enable garden and kitchen vegetable waste to decompose quickly and efficiently. The optimum size is thought to be 1.8 m (6 ft) square and 1.5 m (5 ft) high. For the majority of small gardens, however, this is far too large; it is also too high and difficult for many gardeners to fill. It would also hold more compostable material than a small garden could produce within six months or so.

A compromise size – one that has been found to be efficient – is 1.2 m (4 ft) square and high; the height can be increased to 1.5 m (5 ft) if desired. This is ideal if you are making a three-section bin (see right). If you are making just a single bin, the size can be increased slightly.

Economic design

Constructing three bins right next to each other is less expensive than making three separate compost holders, because it saves on the timber needed for two sides. It is also a stronger construction than a single-bin type.

WHY THREE BINS?

When a three-bin system is up and running, the first bin is being filled with fresh garden and kitchen waste, the second has been filled and the material in it is decomposing, and the third is full of rich compost that is ready for use in the garden. When empty, the third becomes the first, and so on.

Choosing the right wood

The most environmentally friendly timber to use is wood that has been recycled. Timber yards often have reclaimed timber; alternatively, visit salvage and reclamation yards. Some telephone directories have sections that are devoted to sourcing used timber.

Timber that has been pressure-treated with a wood preservative gives the longest possible life, but make sure that it is plant-friendly and will not contaminate the compost with toxic chemicals.

THREE-PART COMPOST BIN

This is the most efficient and timber-saving design to choose when constructing a compost bin. Position it on well-drained, level soil.

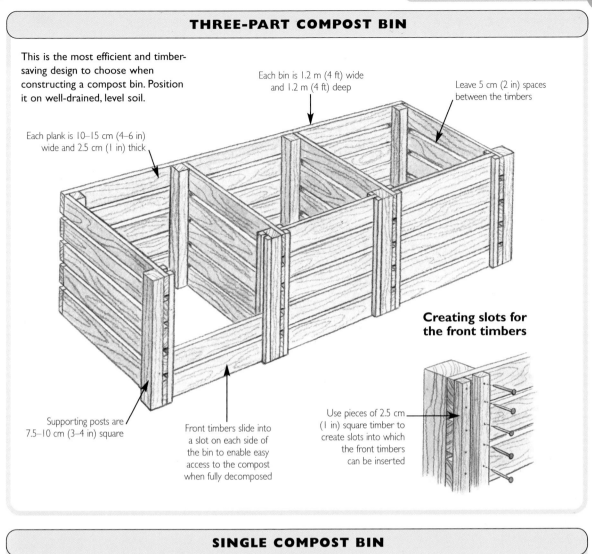

Each bin is 1.2 m (4 ft) wide and 1.2 m (4 ft) deep

Leave 5 cm (2 in) spaces between the timbers

Each plank is 10–15 cm (4–6 in) wide and 2.5 cm (1 in) thick

Supporting posts are 7.5–10 cm (3–4 in) square

Front timbers slide into a slot on each side of the bin to enable easy access to the compost when fully decomposed

Creating slots for the front timbers

Use pieces of 2.5 cm (1 in) square timber to create slots into which the front timbers can be inserted

SINGLE COMPOST BIN

Single compost bins are usually slightly larger than one compartment of a three-part bin (see above).

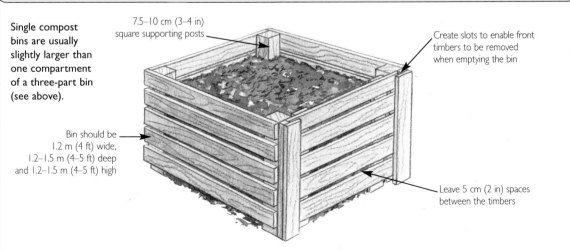

7.5–10 cm (3–4 in) square supporting posts

Create slots to enable front timbers to be removed when emptying the bin

Bin should be 1.2 m (4 ft) wide, 1.2–1.5 m (4–5 ft) deep and 1.2–1.5 m (4–5 ft) high

Leave 5 cm (2 in) spaces between the timbers

Compost bins for nothing

Is recycling easy?

Bin 'improvisation' is both environmentally friendly and a highly satisfying way to create a compost bin. Not using prime materials saves you money and helps to conserve the planet's resources, while creating something from nothing will extend your imagination and involve you in the therapeutic fun of using a few basic do-it-yourself skills. A vast range of structures can be created, modified or adapted, and you can use many earlier cast-aside gardening materials.

EXAMPLES OF IMPROVISED BINS

Look around any garden or allotment and the chances are that there are pensioned-off materials waiting to be used, or take a trip to recycling centres or scrapyards and see what is available. Here are many ideas for creating a compost bin for nothing, together with notes about their advantages and disadvantages.

Disused beehive
- **What to do:** Discard the base and stack the sides on the soil; retain the lid and, if possible, add hinges to it.
- **Advantages:** Quickly and easily constructed; creates an informal, cottage-garden appearance.
- **Disadvantages:** Wood eventually decays, but can be treated with a plant- and bug-friendly preservative.

Plastic water tank
- **What to do:** Use a drill and padsaw to cut out about one-third of the base; drill ventilation holes in the sides and stand in position on the soil.
- **Advantages:** Easily prepared for use.
- **Disadvantages:** Compost needs regular turning to ensure that air reaches the centre of the tank; needs to be covered; best reserved for an allotment.

Car tyres
- **What to do:** Position a tyre on the soil, fill with compost and progressively add further ones to about five tyres high; a lid is needed.
- **Advantages:** Old tyres are readily available.
- **Disadvantages:** Difficult for air to reach the decomposing compost; not aesthetically pleasing and best used on an allotment; requires a lid.

Wooden pallet
- **What to do:** Disassemble a pallet, and nail or screw the edges to form a four-sided cage.
- **Advantages:** Inexpensive, and pallets are easily obtainable; compost is well aerated.
- **Disadvantages:** Sides need secure fixings to prevent them breaking away; cold during winter (insulate with a straw jacket); requires a lid.

EXAMPLES OF IMPROVISED BINS (CONTINUED)

Circular wire bin
- **What to do:** Use a piece of 16-gauge galvanized or plastic-covered wire-netting, about 90 cm (3 ft) wide, to make a bin 0.9–1.2 m (3–4 ft) across. Secure the ends of the netting together, stand upright and use four strong stakes to hold it in position.
- **Advantages:** Cheap and quick to make; air can reach the compost.
- **Disadvantages:** Cold during winter (insulate with a straw jacket); compost tends to dry quickly; requires a covering.

Square wire bin
- **What to do:** Use a piece of 16-gauge galvanized or plastic-covered wire-netting, about 90 cm (3 ft) wide, to form a square bin 0.9–1.2 m (3–4 ft) across, or a rectangular one about 90 cm (3 ft) across and 1.2 m (4 ft) long. Use strong stakes at the corners.
- **Advantages:** Cheap and quick to make; air can reach the compost.
- **Disadvantages:** Cold during winter (insulate with a straw jacket); requires a covering; not as strong and rigid as a circular type.

Wattle hurdles
- **What to do:** Secure 0.9–1.2 m (3–4 ft) high wattle hurdles to form an enclosed 1.5–1.8 m (5–6 ft) square. Use strong supporting stakes at the corners.
- **Advantages:** Quickly assembled; traditional rustic appearance; allows air to reach the compost.
- **Disadvantages:** Not rigid; often short-lived; requires a covering.

Old chestnut palings
- **What to do:** Bend the palings to form an enclosure about 90 cm (3 ft) wide and 1.2 m (4 ft) long; secure to a strong supporting post at each corner.
- **Advantages:** Inexpensive and quick to construct from old fencing; allows air to reach the compost.
- **Disadvantages:** Cold during winter (insulate with a straw jacket); requires a covering.

Concrete blocks
- **What to do:** Stack concrete blocks 0.9–1.2 m (3–4 ft) high to form a three-sided enclosure, and about a similar size in length and width.
- **Advantages:** Keeps the compost moist and warm in winter; can be disassembled quickly.
- **Disadvantages:** Needs a moveable front and a covering.

Carpet
- **What to do:** Cut a piece of carpet into a strip 75–90 cm (2½–3 ft) wide and long enough to form a circle 90 cm (3 ft) across; secure it to 4–5 strong stakes.
- **Advantages:** Cheap and quick to construct.
- **Disadvantages:** Short-term solution; compost remains cold in winter; needs a covering.

Hybrid bins
Often an eclectic medley of materials is used to form a bin; these can include old wire-netting, wooden posts, planks of wood and straw.

Creating a compost heap

How should I start?

Encouraging organic garden and kitchen waste to decompose in a compost heap is the traditional method, while in recent times enclosed plastic bins (see pages 28 and 41) have become popular, especially with home gardeners with small gardens. If you have a large garden with plenty of room, and lots of compostable material, a heap is the best option. The process of creating and filling a compost heap is described here.

STARTING THE COMPOST HEAP

Choosing a position for your compost heap is described on pages 26–27.
Here is step-by-step advice on creating the heap.

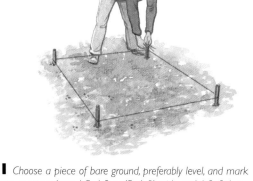

1 *Choose a piece of bare ground, preferably level, and mark out an area about 1.5–1.8 m (5–6 ft) wide and 1.8–2.4 m (6–8 ft) long. This is slightly larger than the area later needed for the compost heap.*

2 *Use a garden fork to dig the soil to about 25 cm (10 in) deep. This loosens compacted soil and enables soil organisms and creatures to enter the compost. It also allows torrential rain to drain away rapidly.*

3 *Rake the area level and use string to mark out an area 1.2–1.5 m (4–5 ft) wide and about 1.8 m (6 ft) long; this can be slightly longer if there is a large amount of garden and kitchen organic waste to be composted.*

4 *If possible, place a 10–15 cm (4–6 in) thick layer of straw over the ground. Thoroughly water this layer and then add garden and kitchen waste in a 10–15 cm (4–6 in) thick layer evenly over the straw.*

STARTING THE COMPOST HEAP (CONTINUED)

5 *For details of the garden and kitchen materials that can and cannot be used, see pages 14–25. Where leftover food is added (and especially if mainly fish and meat), put this towards the centre of the heap.*

6 *Mix up the ingredients and, when the layer is complete, water it thoroughly and tread it down. Then spread a 2.5 cm (1 in) thick layer of garden soil over the vegetable waste. If the soil is acid, dust it with ground limestone (see below).*

7 *Add a further 10–15 cm (4–6 in) thick layer of garden and kitchen waste. Water it thoroughly, tread down and, again, spread a 2.5 cm (1 in) layer of soil over the surface. Add a further dusting of ground limestone, if needed.*

8 *When the heap is about 1.2 m (4 ft) high, thoroughly water the top layer and add a 2.5 cm (1 in) thick layer of soil. Cover the compost heap with a polythene sheet (preferably black) to help retain warmth.*

AFTERCARE

- Regularly check that the compost is moist (see pages 12–13); be prepared to remove the cover and thoroughly water the material.
- After about six weeks (if the compost heap was completed in summer), use a garden fork to turn the heap over. If it was completed in winter, leave this for about 10 weeks.
- After turning over the heap and levelling the top, add further soil to the surface and replace the cover.
- The time needed for the material to decompose and be ready for use varies from summer to winter; always check that the compost fits the description of what it should look like when ready to be used (see pages 12–13).

How much ground limestone?
Where the soil is acid, spread 136 g per m² (4 oz per sq yd) of ground limestone over each layer of soil.

How much sulphate of ammonia?
If sulphate of ammonia is needed (because manure is not available) dust it over the surface of the waste material at 15–30 g per m² (½–1 oz per sq yd). However, rather than measuring out such small quantities, just lightly dust the surface with it.

Why add a layer of garden soil?
Garden soil contains bacteria which quickly multiply and help in the decomposition process. Use friable soil from the top 10–15 cm (4–6 in), not subsoil, which contains more bacteria.

Should I also add manure?
If possible, mix in farmyard manure or droppings and bedding from pets such as rabbits and guinea pigs. If manure is not available, add a light dusting of the nitrogenous fertilizer sulphate of ammonia over the waste material and before a layer of soil is added. Do not mix the sulphate of ammonia and ground limestone together; always add the ground limestone (if needed) to the surface of a layer of soil.

Other ways to compost waste organic material

- In a compost bin (see pages 40–41)
- Quick composting in a compost tumbler or low-framed compost bin (see pages 30–31)
- Compost trenches and holes (see page 29)

Using a compost bin

Is filling a compost bin easy?

Because many households do not produce vast amounts of material to be composted, a compost bin (especially an enclosed plastic type) is more practical than a compost heap (see pages 38–39). Using a compost bin is simplicity itself. As and when organic waste material from kitchens and gardens becomes available, just put it in the bin. An alternative for smaller households is to have a wormery (see pages 48–53).

FREQUENTLY ASKED QUESTIONS

How many types of compost bin are there?

There are two main types.
- The first resembles a compost heap (see pages 38–39). However, instead of being built without any constriction along its sides, it is usually constrained by a wood, wire-netting, brick or breeze-block surround. A range of these compost bins is illustrated on pages 32–37 and includes shop-bought types, home-made ones and those constructed from recycled materials. This type of compost bin is best filled in the same way as recommended for compost heaps (see pages 38–39).
- The second is fully enclosed, usually made of a plastic-type material and with a lid; a range of these compost bins is shown on pages 32–33. This type of bin is ideal for households which each week have only a limited amount of material to be composted (filling this type of compost bin is described on the opposite page).

Should I always keep the lid on the bin?

Yes, as it helps to keep the compost moist and prevent rodents being attracted to the material, especially if leftover meals of fish and meat are added. The lid also prevents flies becoming a problem in summer.

Can I use a redundant plastic dustbin?

Yes. Local authorities are increasingly providing residents with 'wheelie bins' for the collection of both recyclable and landfill materials, making plastic dustbins redundant. See page 33 for how to convert one.

Can I use a redundant metal dustbin?

Yes, just cut out the base and put the bin in position. However, because the bin is made of metal, the compost will warm up rapidly in summer and may need regular watering. In winter, however, the compost will remain cooler than in a plastic bin. Covering the bin with a piece of old carpet helps to overcome this problem.

How can I prevent the lid being blown off?

Strong, gusting wind – as well as inquisitive squirrels – can remove lids. If this happens, tie a brick to one end of a short piece of thin rope, with the other end tied to a handle in the lid. If a handle is not present, carefully drill a 6 mm (¼ in) hole in the lid's top, pass one end of the rope through it and tie a thick knot. The brick will hang down at the bin's side and ensure that the lid remains shut.

Is a door at the base of a plastic compost bin essential?

This is not essential, although if all the contents of a bin are totally decomposed and ready to be used it is an advantage. However, if you are uncertain about the contents – and this is influenced by the time of year, size of the compost bin and the regularity with which material is put into it – it is easier to lift off the entire compost bin, remove all the totally decomposed compost, and put the remaining material back in the bin.

Two examples of compost bins with trap doors at their bases are shown on page 33.

POSITIONING AND FILLING AN ENCLOSED PLASTIC COMPOST BIN

Step 7
After about six months (longer if the mixture was started in winter), carefully lift away the bin to reveal the compost. Remove the material at the base which is decomposed and ready to be used (see pages 12–13).

Step 6
The material can be left without turning. If in summer the compost appears to be dry, add water to the mixture and thoroughly soak it. In winter, you can place an insulative jacket around the bin to keep the compost warm.

Step 8
Replace the compost bin in its position and return to it the material that is not yet decomposed. Then continue adding garden and kitchen waste in the same way as before.

Step 5
Newspapers and used kitchen paper towels can be added, but not excessively. Do not exceed an equal parts mixture of paper and vegetable waste and always first shred the paper, rather than forming a thick, dense layer.

Step 1
Fork over a piece of soil to loosen its surface, enabling soil organisms and creatures to enter the compost bin when put in position. This also ensures that water from heavy rainstorms drains rapidly.

Step 4
Materials that can and cannot be added to a compost bin are detailed on pages 14–23. Do not create dense layers of a single type (such as lawn mowings), and always chop up thick stems to enable them to decompose rapidly.

Step 2
A plastic compost bin will have an open base. Stand it directly on the soil, ensuring it is firm, level and upright. If it becomes twisted and distorted, the lid may not easily fit.

Step 3
If possible, add a 7.5–10 cm (3–4 in) layer of straw or hay to the base. Then toss kitchen and garden organic waste into the bin as it becomes available. Try to keep the surface of the material level.

Troubleshooting

As you will have already seen, the decomposition of organic waste in a compost heap or bin is influenced by several factors, including the nature of the material put into it, the weather, the time of year and its size, and sometimes a few problems can occur. These include the compost heap remaining inactive, giving off obnoxious smells and attracting rodents. All these problems can be solved and here is a troubleshooting guide to correcting them.

Are there many problems?

Usually, compost heaps and compost bins are easy to look after, but problems occasionally arise.

With experience, you will quickly notice problems as they arise and be able to cure them. The decomposition process and the influence of environmental factors are discussed on pages 12–13. Here are some of the problems that might occur, together with ways to correct them.

COMPOST HEAP APPEARS TO BE INACTIVE

This is caused by several factors, including the compost being too dry or wet, or an incorrect balance of materials (see pages 14–19 for suitable ingredients, pages 38–39 for creating a compost heap, and pages 40–41 for looking after a compost bin). Here are a few common reasons why the compost might be inactive.

- **Compost has finished decomposing:** At this stage, it will be brown and crumbly, with the individual stems, leaves and other materials earlier put into the heap or bin being unrecognizable. There will be no obnoxious smells and the material can be either cool or slightly warm. It is then ready to be used in a garden.
- **Insufficient nitrogen:** A lack of nitrogen-rich material in the heap will reduce or even stop decomposition. Therefore, you should try to mix in animal manure and grass cuttings (both in thin layers). In addition, add in urine-soaked litter from family pets such as rabbits and guinea pigs. Poultry manure is also rich in nitrogen and ideal for 'activating' the heap; ensure it is spread out and used in thin layers.

Forking over a compost heap enables air to enter the mixture, encouraging more rapid decomposition.

- **Insufficient oxygen:** Air is essential for microbial life in a compost heap and without oxygen it becomes smelly. Fork over the heap to enable air to enter, and put the decomposing material in thin layers, especially those such as grass cuttings which become compacted when wet.
- **Insufficient moisture:** Moisture is essential for microbial life. Apart from a visual check of the compost, a test for sufficient moisture involves slightly burrowing into the heap to check if it is moist and that the many compost creatures are active. Another test is to squeeze a handful of compost; if a few drops of moisture escape, the moisture content is right. If necessary, thoroughly water the material.

Squeeze a handful of compost to test for moisture content.

- **Cold weather:** Microbial life is inhibited by low temperatures. Low winter temperatures are a problem, especially if the compost heap or bin is full of material waiting to start its decomposing process. Fork over the heap and add nitrogen-rich material (see opposite), water the material and cover. In very cold winter, decomposition may not begin until spring, when temperatures rise dramatically.

COMPOST HEAP REMAINS DRY AND INACTIVE

Thoroughly wet the compost and cover it.

COMPOST REMAINS DAMP AND WARM, BUT ONLY IN THE MIDDLE

Usually a result of the compost heap being too small; it especially occurs in winter. Form a compost heap at least 90 cm (3 ft) high and wide, and cover it to prevent cold rain and snow reaching and cooling the compost.

MATTED MATERIAL IS NOT DECOMPOSING

Thick layers of single types, especially newspapers and grass cuttings, are slow to decompose as they both exclude air and prevent water spreading to layers below. The immediate

solution is to fork over the heap and break up congested layers. Subsequently, only add thin layers of these materials.

THE RESULTING COMPOST IS LESS THAN EXPECTED

This is normal, since compost heaps reduce by as much as 60 per cent during decomposition.

THERE IS A STRONG, UNPLEASANT SMELL RESEMBLING AMMONIA

Usually results from excessive amounts of waste cooked food (especially meat and fish) being added in thick layers. Fork over the heap to spread these scraps and add shredded newspapers, straw and hay.

THERE ARE SMELLS OF RANCID BUTTER AND ROTTEN EGGS

These smells arise from insufficient oxygen in the heap to encourage the activities of microbial life that is essential for decomposition. Compaction and the compost heap being too wet are the prime causes. Fork over the heap, add materials such as straw or hay to soak up excess water, and cover to prevent rain making the problem worse.

IT IS ATTRACTING RODENTS

These pests are mainly attracted by kitchen scraps and especially uneaten meals containing a high proportion of meat or fish. If the latter are added to a compost heap, break them up and place them in the centre. Alternatively, use a rodent-proof compost bin.

IT IS ATTRACTING FLIES

Flies are especially attracted to uneaten meals. Therefore, add these scraps to the centre of the heap and cover with other compostable materials. Alternatively, use a bin with a cover.

IT IS ATTRACTING INSECTS AND OTHER CREATURES

See pages 8–9 for those that are beneficial to gardens.

Covering an open-topped compost bin prevents the ingredients becoming either too dry or too wet.

Mixing compost with the soil

Does garden compost make any difference to soil?

Compost is invaluable in gardens, adding plant foods, improving the soil's structure and helping to create a 'green' environment. Unlike stable manure, which usually has to be bought, organic garden and kitchen waste is readily available and can be easily converted into a material that improves garden soil. To achieve this, you can either dig it into the soil (usually during autumn and winter digging) or spread it as a mulch.

DO ALL VEGETABLES BENEFIT FROM GARDEN COMPOST?

All plants benefit from having decomposed garden compost mixed with the soil during digging, as it improves its fertility and structure (see below), but some vegetables benefit more than others, especially those that produce large amounts of leafy growth. Therefore, vegetable plots are best divided into three to enable a three-year cycle of plants to be achieved. This 'crop rotation' is described on page 46.

Potatoes, whether grown in vegetable plots or containers on a patio, produce good crops when the soil is enriched with high-quality garden compost.

Lettuces, with their leafy growth, will benefit from garden compost.

Benefits of garden compost to the soil

- It provides plant foods, with the bonus of including many trace elements necessary for balanced and healthy growth.

- It improves drainage, thereby enabling soil to warm up earlier in spring. This is especially beneficial in clay soil, which tends to be cold and badly drained.

- It darkens the soil, enabling it to absorb more warmth from the sun (useful in spring to encourage the early growth of plants).

- It improves sandy soils by enabling them to retain more moisture.

- It creates a healthy and active environment for beneficial soil bacteria and creatures, including worms.

- It is a natural way to improve soil and prevents the build-up of toxic chemicals that either remain in the soil or drain through into ditches and streams.

SINGLE DIGGING

Divide the plot down the middle of its length. Take out one 'spit' or 'trench' – the depth and width of the spade – from the first half and lay the soil down on one side. Add manure or compost to the trench bottom. Remove annual weeds from the second trench and place them upside-down in the first trench. Take out the soil from the second trench to the depth of one spit and lay it over the weeds in the first trench. Rerun the procedure down to the end of the plot. Move to the second half and continue. When you get to the end of the second half, put the contents of the first spit that you dug into the last trench.

Pros – The close contact with the soil tells you a lot about its quality.
Cons – The activity is rather time-consuming.

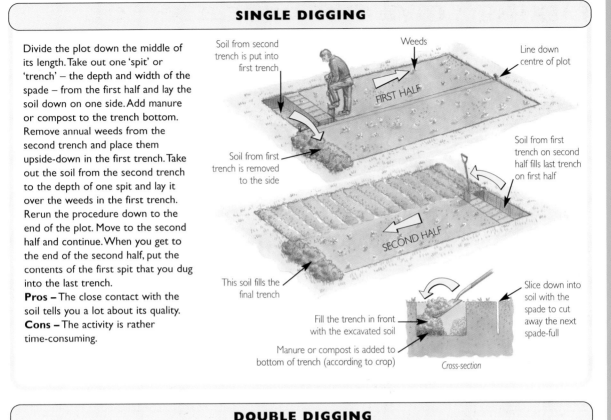

Soil from second trench is put into first trench

Weeds

Line down centre of plot

FIRST HALF

Soil from first trench is removed to the side

Soil from first trench on second half fills last trench on first half

SECOND HALF

This soil fills the final trench

Fill the trench in front with the excavated soil

Manure or compost is added to bottom of trench (according to crop)

Slice down into soil with the spade to cut away the next spade-full

Cross-section

DOUBLE DIGGING

Divide the plot down the middle of its length. Take out two 'spits' – so as to finish up with a trench about 60 cm (2 ft) wide – and lay the soil down on one side. Add manure or compost to the trench bottom and turn it over to the full depth of a fork. Skim the turf about 5 cm (2 in) deep from the next two spits and lay it upside-down in the first trench. Take out the soil from the next two spits and lay it over the turf so as to fill up the first trench. Repeat the procedure down to the end of the plot. Move to the second half and continue. When you get to the end of the second half, put the contents of the first two spits that you dug into the last trench.

Pros – Although the soil is broken up to two spits deep, the subsoil remains undisturbed.
Cons – It is very hard work.

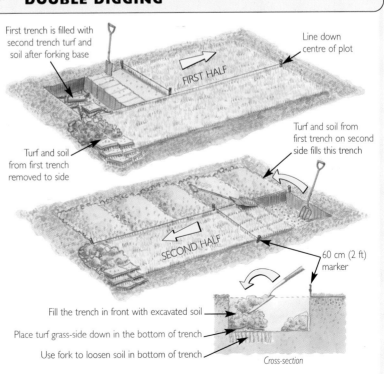

First trench is filled with second trench turf and soil after forking base

Line down centre of plot

FIRST HALF

Turf and soil from first trench removed to side

Turf and soil from first trench on second side fills this trench

SECOND HALF

60 cm (2 ft) marker

Fill the trench in front with excavated soil

Place turf grass-side down in the bottom of trench

Use fork to loosen soil in bottom of trench

Cross-section

Digging and crop rotation

*When should
I dig in
compost?*

To get the most benefit from garden compost, it needs to be mixed with soil at the right time. Some crops especially benefit from having their roots in garden compost or well-decomposed manure recently added to the soil. For this reason, vegetable plots are usually divided into three parts to enable vegetables with similar needs to be grown in the same area. Each year, each area has a different crop, but in strict rotation. For 'single' and 'double' digging, see page 45.

GETTING THE GROUPINGS RIGHT

Divide the vegetable plot into three parts, so that each year the groupings of vegetables can be rotated. Each group has separate needs and times when garden compost or manure is dug into the soil. For example:

• **Root vegetables:** Dig the soil in winter, but do not add garden compost or manure. Also, do not apply lime. About two weeks before sowing or planting, rake a general-purpose fertilizer into the soil.

• **Brassicas:** Dig the soil in winter, adding garden compost or manure, especially if the soil is lacking in humus. If the soil is acid, apply lime, but not at the same time as digging in manure or compost. Apply lime, if needed, about two weeks later. Then, around two weeks before sowing or planting, rake a general-purpose fertilizer into the soil.

• **Legumes and salad crops:** Dig the soil in winter and add copious amounts of well-decayed garden compost or manure. If the soil is acid, apply lime, but not at the same time as digging and mixing in the compost or manure. Apply a dusting of lime, if needed, about two weeks later. In a further two weeks and before sowing or planting, rake a general-purpose fertilizer into the soil.

LARGE NUMBERS OF POTATOES

In small gardens, potatoes are invariably put in the same group as 'root vegetables'. However, when growing large numbers of potatoes, they can be grown in a four-year cycle and slotted in between 'brassicas' and 'root vegetables'; give them the same soil preparation as for 'root vegetables'.

GETTING THE ROTATION RIGHT

When starting to grow vegetables it is initially difficult to get the rotation right, but after a few years adopt the following sequence:

ROOT

LEGUMES AND SALADS

BRASSICAS

Mulches and raised beds

The primary role of mulching is to cover the soil to reduce the loss of moisture through evaporation from the ground's surface, and to suppress the growth of weeds. A mulch also helps insulate the roots of plants from extremes of temperature. Organic mulches add nutrients to the soil, as well as helping to prevent torrential rain bouncing off muddy ground and splattering plants with dirty soil. Mulching also assists in preventing soil erosion.

What is mulching?

PREPARING TO MULCH PLANTS

This is best undertaken in spring or early summer.
- Hoe off or pull up annual weeds (see pages 18–19) and add them to a compost heap or bin.
- Fork up perennial weeds (see pages 22–23) and either put them on a bonfire or in a thick polythene bag (see page 22).
- If the soil's surface is hard and crusty, use a hoe or garden fork to break it up. This will enable moisture to percolate into the lower soil.

Spread the mulch between the plants, but not touching them.

- Thoroughly moisten the soil. If a mulch is put on top of dry soil, the ground will remain dry and impede the spread and growth of roots.
- Spread well-decomposed compost over the soil, but not touching plants. A thickness of 7.5–10 cm (3–4 in) is desirable.

WHAT HAPPENS TO THE MULCH?

Throughout summer, the mulch will be drawn into the ground by soil creatures, including worms. In the following spring, hoe the remains of the mulch into the soil's surface before adding a further layer.

RAISED BEDS

What are raised beds?
Raised beds are no more than little enclosures that allow you to raise the soil up above the level of the underlying ground. Details of decorative raised beds are given on page 75, while those on this page are for growing vegetables.

Advantages of raised beds
Raising and containing the soil is a good option on at least five counts – you do not have to stoop so low, you do not need to step on the soil, the plants are to some extent protected from pests, the soil in the bed can be modified to suit the plants, and the sides of the bed make it easier to keep out weeds.

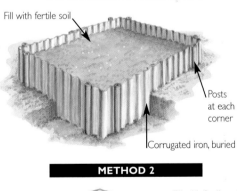

METHOD 1

Fill with fertile soil

Posts at each corner

Corrugated iron, buried

☛ Use corrugated plastic or metal sheeting to create a bed. Dig the sheeting deep into the soil so that the wavy end is uppermost. Support it with posts banged into the ground. This is a good option for keeping invasive plants such as mint in, and creeping weeds out. You could cover the sharp edge of the corrugated sheeting with strips of wood or plastic.

METHOD 2

Fill with fertile soil

Lengths of wood nailed or bolted together

☛ Use large-section wood to build a heavy frame that sits on the ground. You could use short lengths of railway sleeper, or perhaps lengths of salvaged wood. Building sites are a good source for offcuts of ceiling and floor joists.

What is a wormery?

How do worms create compost?

When vegetable waste is composted in a traditional compost heap in a garden, the temperature rises at its centre to a point when it is too hot for anything but bacteria to live. This is sometimes known as 'hot' composting. Low-temperature composting is possible in a 'wormery', however. Here a specific type of worm can be encouraged to turn small quantities of vegetable waste at a time into high-quality compost for use in gardens.

WHAT IS VERMICULTURE?

This is the name given to using worms to turn vegetable waste into compost. You might also come across the term 'vermicompost' – this is the material created in a wormery.

WHAT ARE THE SPECIAL WORMS NEEDED FOR A WORMERY?

Variously known as red worms, manure worms, red wigglers, brandlings, tiger worms and fish worms, these worms are naturally found in decaying organic material, manure heaps and piles of leaves. They are usually 5–10 cm (2–4 in) long, and rarely found in garden soil. Properly known as *Eisenia foetida* (sometimes *Eisenia fetida*), they are buff-red and gain their scientific name from the way in which, when handled roughly, they defend themselves by exuding a pungent liquid. The traditional garden worm is not suitable for a wormery.

Brandlings or tiger worms

Soil-living earthworm

WHERE CAN I GET THE WORMS?

They are readily available through vermiculture companies (mainly by mail order) and fishing-tackle shops. When starting, you will need about 1,000 worms, which is about 500 g (1 lb), to ensure that the composting process is as quick as it can be. They are sometimes sold as 'starter' kits, and the worms are marketed by weight rather than number.

WHAT ARE THE NEEDS OF THE WORMS?

To keep them active and happy, they need a dark, moist (not waterlogged) and warm area, preferably 13–24°C (55–75°F). They dislike temperatures in excess of 27°C (80°F) and will die at 32°C (90°F) or higher. Conversely, they will become inactive at low temperatures.

TIERED WORMERY

Close-fitting lid keeps out rain and vermin

Top tray partly full of recently added and broken-up kitchen and garden organic waste

When this material has been removed, the empty tray is placed on top of the wormery

Base unit with strong legs

Tap at the base enables collection of the liquid that accumulates; it can be used in a garden or added to compost in a heap or bin

Moisture-mat to keep the decomposing organic waste and worms warm and slightly moist

Middle tray containing organic material in the process of being broken down by worms

Bottom tray contains decomposed material that is ready for removal and using in a garden (most worms have migrated upwards and are working on material in the trays above)

Proprietary wormeries formed of several trays enable the compost to be harvested easily. The trays are perforated to allow the worms to move between them. Height: 73 cm (29 in), width: 50 cm (20 in).

The worms dislike extremely acidic conditions and if this occurs, perhaps through the addition of too much citrus fruit such as lemon peel, add a dusting of calcified seaweed.

HOW ACTIVE ARE THE WORMS?

They reproduce rapidly and if you start with 500 g (1 lb) of worms they become 1 kg (2 lb) within 3–4 months. They do need a regular food source (about three times their own weight of food each week), however, and a suitable environment (see opposite page). They are known to have a life span of four years, although this is usually less when regularly disturbed in a wormery.

HOW LONG DOES DECOMPOSITION TAKE?

The rate of decomposition depends on the number of worms, the temperature (see opposite page), and the amount of vegetable waste added at one time. This should be 'little and often', rather than providing the worms with a mass of material which they cannot quickly process.

WILL THE WORMS COME TO HARM IF THERE IS A DELAY IN ADDING FURTHER VEGETABLE WASTE?

They can live for several weeks without any problem if they have exhausted the supply and additional food is not added. If you go away on holiday, for example, they should be fine.

WILL IT BECOME SMELLY?

Usually, the composting process does not produce bad smells. However, problems may occur if:
- The composting bin is overloaded: stop filling it and gently stir the contents to enable more air to penetrate. Do not add further compostable material until the smell disappears.
- The drainage hole (or holes) in the bin are blocked, causing the mixture to become excessively moist. Check the holes regularly and unblock them if necessary, but remember that the mixture must not become dry.
- The material is too acidic. If this happens, cut down on adding acidic fruit waste (such as grapefruit and orange).

WHAT DO I NEED TO START WITH?

The four basics are:
- A composting bin, usually made of plastic or wood.
- Worms (see opposite page for starter weight and numbers).
- Bedding (ranges from corrugated cardboard and shredded newspaper to leaves).
- Kitchen and garden vegetable waste.
See pages 52–53 for details of getting your wormery started.

WILL IT ATTRACT FLIES?

Harmless fruit flies sometimes appear if you overload the bin (in which case there will be a large amount of waste still to be processed by the worms), so try not to add too much material at any one time. Covering the surface with newspapers (which keeps the compost damp) will also help to deter the fruit flies. If the problem continues, try moving the bin into a new position where the flies will not annoy you.

Fruit flies are harmless

WILL THE COMPOSTING PROCESS ATTRACT VERMIN?

To decrease the risk of rodents becoming interested in the decomposing material, only add vegetable waste to the bin, not left-over cooked meats (these produce offensive odours, which are attractive to vermin), oily foods or grains, and dairy products.

Try to avoid attracting rodents

HOW OFTEN DO I NEED TO HARVEST THE COMPOST?

Usually once or twice a year, although initially this depends on the number of worms added to the bin.

IS HARVESTING THE COMPOST DIFFICULT?

Removing the fully composted material is easy, although the technique you should use depends on whether you want to empty the bin completely or only remove part of the compost (see pages 52–53 for details). In basic terms, it is just a matter of separating the worms from the compost.

WHAT CAN I DO WITH THE COMPOSTED MATERIAL?

There are many uses for the rich garden compost created in a wormery, from mulching the soil's surface to mixing it with soil when digging (see pages 44–47 for details).

The inside of a wormery is filled with trays of organic material that the worms transform into compost through their digestive system.

Making a wormery

What is the best way to make a wormery?

It is quick and easy to create a wormery. All you need is a compost bin (shop-bought or home-made), usually made of plastic or (for some home-made types) wood, the special worms (see pages 48–49), and organic kitchen and garden waste for them to digest and turn into compost. This compost can be used for several purposes, including mulching the soil's surface (see page 46) and for digging into the ground (see pages 44–45).

SUITABLE CONTAINERS

In addition to making your own wormery (out of an old plastic dustbin or some wood), there are many proprietary wormeries available from garden centres or specialist vermiculture companies trading on the internet.

Shop-bought wormeries

These include plastic bin types, where the wormery is filled and emptied from above. Their internal structure resembles that of home-made ones (see opposite for one adapted from a plastic dustbin). These shop-bought types are available in several sizes, from a capacity of 20 litres (4.4 gallons) that is suitable for a single person or to nurture a child's interest in gardening, to 100 litres (22 gallons) – ideal for a large family. It is worth remembering that only a limited amount of organic kitchen and garden waste can be added to a wormery at one time and, therefore, its size needs to be in proportion to the amount of waste that is regularly available.

Tiered wormeries

These are invariably shop-bought and take two main forms: those with a rectangular and tray-like structure, and circular types. Both types have their devotees and advantages, but for many wormery enthusiasts the rectangular shape is better as it offers a larger surface area in which the worms can operate. For details about filling tiered wormeries, see pages 52–53.

Square, tiered wormeries mounted on legs are ideal for gardens as well as in garages. Ensure that a drain tap is present.

If legs are not present, put the wormery where the drain tap can be easily used with a container placed beneath it.

Tiered wormeries are formed of several sections, which are easy to assemble.

HOME-MADE WORMERY, USING A PLASTIC DUSTBIN

Always thoroughly clean the dustbin with soap and water before modifying; rinse several times with clean water.

Easily removable but secure lid

Height: 73 cm (29 in)
Width: 50 cm (20 in)

Worms: initially they need to be placed on 'bedding material', such as shredded newspaper, leafmould or decomposed garden compost

Ring of 6–12 mm (¼–½ in) drainage holes drilled around the base, about 5 cm (2 in) above the bin's base

Layer of several newspapers to keep the decomposing organic waste and worms warm and slightly moist

Organic kitchen or garden waste, chopped up to encourage rapid decomposition

Thick and rigid divider board, drilled with 12–18 mm (½–¾ in) holes to enable excess moisture to drain

5–7.5 cm (2–3 in) layer of clean gravel or small pebbles in the bin's base

USING A WOODEN BOX

Some of the earliest wormeries were wooden boxes and it is still a good and inexpensive way to create a wormery. Here are the basics. See pages 52–53 for how to fill the box with bedding material and worms.

You will need a box made of strong wood that has not been painted with a chemical wood preservative. However, a coating with a non-chemical preservative, such as linseed oil, will extend the life of the wood. Thick plywood is an excellent material to use as it retains its shape, even when constantly damp.

Drill several 3–6 mm (⅛–¼ in) wide holes in the base for drainage and aeration. Drill further ones around the sides to ensure oxygen can enter the box to enable the worms to breathe.

Place the box in a garage or, in summer, a sheltered and shady position outdoors, where it will not be in direct sunlight.

A box with a large surface area is ideal: 30 cm (1 ft) deep, 90 cm (3 ft) long and 60 cm (2 ft) wide.

A hinged or easily removable lid is essential. It needs to be secure and (if the wormery is positioned outside) able to prevent rain entering the box. It also needs to keep the worms warm and to retain them within the box. A thick lid will prevent the box becoming excessively warm in summer (see pages 48–49 for the temperatures needed to keep the worms active and happy).

A drip-tray is essential to catch moisture escaping from the box; position the box on bricks so that the base is slightly raised above the drip-tray and will not be constantly standing in moisture.

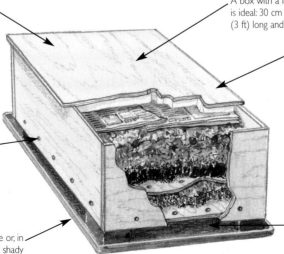

Using a wormery

Apart from the wormery itself and the correct number and type of worms (see pages 48–49), to begin with you will need some material to create 'bedding'. Suitable materials include shredded newspaper, leafmould and decomposed garden compost, all of which are inexpensive and easily obtained. Although the worms do not have immediate appeal for everyone, eventually they can become a fascinating topic of conversation.

WHERE SHOULD I PLACE MY WORMERY?

Positioning the wormery is important, as the worms need warmth (see pages 48–49), and in many climates suitable temperatures are not present outdoors in winter. Therefore, indoors or in a garage are possible places for a wormery, especially in winter, although during summer it can be moved outdoors to a warm but shaded spot. Heavy summer rainstorms can quickly cool the wormery and slow up the activity of the worms, so shelter from rain is also important.

GETTING STARTED WITH A BIN-TYPE WORMERY

If the wormery is home-made from a plastic dustbin (see pages 50–51), ensure the holes in or around its base are not blocked. Stand the bin in a drip-tray. Shop-bought bin types have a drainage tap at the base and this needs to be positioned so that a container can be put under it. Preparing the bin is the same, whether it is home-made or shop-bought.

1 *Fill the base with a 5–7.5 cm (2–3 in) layer of clean gravel or small pebbles. This ensures that the base of the wormery is free-draining, enabling moisture to escape through the drainage holes or tap.*

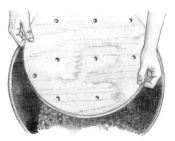

2 *On top of this drainage material place a circular piece of thick, rigid wood, the width of the bin. It must have several 12–18 mm (½–¾ in) holes drilled in it to enable moisture from the worm area to drain. Excessive moisture in the worm chamber is detrimental to the worms.*

3 *Add a 7.5–10 cm (3–4 in) thick layer of shredded newspaper, leafmould or decomposed garden compost. This provides the 'bedding' for the worms.*

4 *Spread the worms (see pages 48–49 for details) on top of the bedding.*

GETTING STARTED WITH A BIN-TYPE WORMERY (CONTINUED)

5 *Add a thin layer of chopped-up kitchen or garden waste. Do not be tempted to form a large and thick layer, as the worms will not be able to cope with it and it may start to decay and smell before they can work on it. Little and often is the clue to success when adding organic kitchen and garden waste.*

6 *Spread a layer of damp newspapers over the surface to keep the worms warm and moist.*

7 *Place the lid in position and leave the bin alone for 2–3 weeks for the worms to settle down.*

LOOKING AFTER YOUR WORMERY

The worms will need regular attention to ensure that they are active.

- Feed them on a variety of chopped-up kitchen and garden waste, but not until they have digested the previously added material.
- Avoid materials such as seeds and diseased material, as well as large amounts of citrus peel. It is also best to avoid leftover fish and meat meals (they smell and attract vermin).
- Give the worms a variety of food, not just one type.
- Keep the lid on the wormery to prevent fruit flies gaining access.
- Do not allow the material to become either dry or too wet. If dry, carefully and evenly add a little water. If the material becomes too wet, add shredded newspaper to soak up the excess moisture.

HARVESTING THE COMPOST

Once or twice a year, whenever the bin fills up, remove the top layer of worms together with kitchen and garden waste that has not been decomposed by them. Place this on one side and remove the composted waste from the bottom of the bin. Then, refill the bin in the way recommended for starting the wormery (see left), adding the worms and uncomposted material in the appropriate layer.

When emptying a wormery bin, separate the decomposed material from the worms and the material they are working on.

Can I store the harvested compost?

If not used immediately, put it in hessian sacks and store in a cool, dry place until needed for mulching or digging in to the soil.

Will the worms come to harm if I go on holiday?

If the worms are fed a few days before you go away, they will not come to any harm on their own for 2–3 weeks. If longer, ask a friend to add a few scraps of varied food for them.

Prodigious multiplication

The worms breed rapidly and within a few months a single worm can produce 1,500 further worms. The more worms there are in a wormery, the faster the organic kitchen and garden waste becomes decomposed.

Filling and looking after a tiered wormery

Because the wormery is formed of separate chambers stacked one upon another (see pages 48 and 50), filling and looking after a tiered wormery is slightly different from maintaining and harvesting material from the bin type (see left).

- The base unit gives support to the tired wormery. When established and the worms have been active for several months, the bottom tray contains decomposed material. The middle tray has organic material the worms are working on, and the top tray is partly full of recently added and broken up kitchen and garden waste, which is waiting to be worked on by the worms.
- The worms have a natural tendency to migrate upwards when they have finished decomposing organic waste in one layer.
- To harvest the composted material, remove and empty the bottom tray and replace it at the top, holding material that is waiting to be digested.

Looking after worms in a wooden box

Fill and maintain the box in the same way as for a bin-type wormery (see left).

What is green manuring?

Does green manuring benefit the soil?

The act of digging the ground and mixing in 'green manure' – specially grown crop plants – improves both the fertility and structure of the soil. It increases aeration, aids the soil's ability to retain water (especially well-drained, sandy soils), and enables excess water to drain away. Some green manure plants also have nitrogen-fixing qualities. Green manuring is an effective, natural way to improve a patch of soil for subsequent plants or crops.

ARE THERE MANY SUITABLE GREEN MANURE PLANTS?

There are several crops to choose from – 11 of them are described and illustrated on pages 56–57. Some of these green manure crops are suitable solely for growing and harvesting in spring and summer, and others are suitable for overwintering. However, a few of them can be grown in both ways (see pages 56–57).

DOES GREEN MANURING IMPROVE BOTH CLAY AND SANDY SOILS?

Both types of soil benefit. With sandy soil, the addition of a green manure crop especially increases its water-retaining properties, as well as increasing its nutritional content. With clay soil, it improves aeration and drainage, as well as adding to its fertility. Green manuring also encourages the presence of beneficial soil bacteria and creatures.

HOW TO DIG A GREEN MANURE CROP INTO THE SOIL

- If the green manure crop is bulky and tall, first cut it down with a scythe or garden shears to make it more manageable.
- When digging in green manure, do not bury it deeply, especially if the soil is mainly formed of clay, badly aerated and poorly drained. The trenches should be only 15–20 cm (6–8 in) deep, to retain air. A lack of air in the soil does not encourage the presence of soil organisms, which are essential for the breaking down of green manure into compounds which plants can readily absorb.
- Spread the material thinly and uniformly in the trenches, to help it decompose more quickly.
- Allow about 2–3 weeks in summer and 4–6 weeks in winter between digging in a green manure crop and planting or sowing a crop on top. This is because bacteria in the soil will be working to break down the material and using nitrogen which otherwise would have been available to young plants. Sowing or planting too early radically diminishes growth.

Spread the green manure evenly

Trench 15–20 cm (6–8 in) deep

MOISTURE DEPLETION

It is claimed that overwintering green manure crops, such as clover, prevent the soil absorbing the essential winter rain that tops up the ground with moisture. On a small, garden scale this is not a problem, because the area can be generously watered either in spring or before another crop is grown on that piece of ground.

DOES THE SOIL'S SURFACE BENEFIT FROM A COVERING OF A GREEN MANURE CROP?

While growing, and before being dug into the soil, a green manure crop has several benefits. These include:

- It prevents torrential rain leaching plant foods, especially in light and sandy soils.
- It keeps soil cool in summer, preventing surface cracking and the roots of plants being damaged.
- It keeps soil warm in winter and is especially beneficial in cold regions.
- It prevents soil erosion from strong winds during hot and dry summers, and from torrential rain in both winter and summer.
- It helps to suppress the growth of weeds.

The medicinal magic of Comfrey

Apart from being an ideal green manure plant, Comfrey (*Symphytum* spp.) is acclaimed for its wide medicinal uses. Commonly known as Knitbone, Knitback, Bruisewort, Healing Herb and Boneset, it has been used to aid the repair of bones, to relieve pain from bruises and to heal wounds. The leaves of Comfrey contain significant amounts of vitamin B12, as well as silica and allantoin, substances which accelerate the replenishment of bone matter and aid the rapid healing of bones and wounds.

Also, an infusion of the roots of Comfrey has been used in cough remedies, for treating asthma and as a gargle to ease sore throats. It is also known in the treatment of diarrhoea and dysentery.

The medicinal qualities of the roots were well known in the seventeenth century by the astrologer-physician Nicholas Culpeper, who used fresh roots of Comfrey in the treatment of gout.

Nitrogen-fixing plants

The use of crops that enrich soil with nitrogen was known to the Greeks and Romans, but it was not until the end of the nineteenth century that the reasons for this became known. Leguminous crops, such as peas, beans and clover, are able to utilize atmospheric nitrogen in their growth, provided that a certain soil bacterium (*Rhizobium*) is in contact with their roots. This bacterium inhabits structures, known as nodules, on the roots of specific plants and it is in these nodules that the nitrogen is stored.

Green manure crops that have this nitrogen-fixing ability are invaluable, because when they are dug into the soil they slowly release nitrogen for the following crop to use. A range of plants with this nitrogen-fixing ability are described and illustrated on pages 56–57.

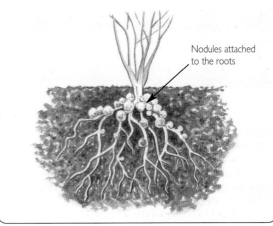

Nodules attached to the roots

Early cure for vertigo

Trigonella foenum-graecum (Fenugreek; see page 57) is said to provide a cure for vertigo when the leaves are bruised and placed on the sufferer's head.

SYMPHYTUM X UPLANDICUM (RUSSIAN COMFREY)

This hardy, herbaceous, low-temperature perennial is a hybrid between *Symphytum asperum* (Prickly Comfrey) and *S. officinale* (Common Comfrey), and is also known as *S. peregrinum*. Unlike *S. officinale*, it rarely produces seed and therefore is more controllable in a small garden.

The plant contains high percentages of nitrogen, calcium and potassium, and can be added to compost heaps to serve as an activator to encourage decay in other compost materials. When using it in this way, break off individual leaves and spread them evenly over the surface of the compost, or directly mix it in with other materials.

Because Russian Comfrey readily decomposes, you can dig it directly into the soil and use it in the same way as a green manure crop. You can also use it as a mulch, when it both creates a surface covering and provides food for plants.

Another way of using this plant is to convert it into a potassium-rich liquid feed. Put the leaves in a strong plastic bucket (with a small hole in its base) and allow the liquid to drain into another plastic container. Before using it as a fertilizer, you must dilute it, using the ratio of 1 part of this liquid to 15 of clean water. Be warned that it has an unpleasant smell.

Green manure plants

Several green-leaved plants can be grown as a green manure crop for later digging into the soil to improve its structure, as well as providing food for the following plants grown on that piece of land. Some of these crops are best sown and grown in spring and summer, whereas others need to be 'overwintered' and dug into the soil in the following year. A few green manure plants are also nitrogen-fixing (see page 55).

THE NATURE OF GREEN MANURE PLANTS

Several green manure plants have specific seasons when they should be sown and, later, dug into the soil. Others are more flexible, and can be sown and used at several times during the year. The plants described here are grouped according to whether they are mainly 'overwintering' types or 'spring and summer' types.

Plants mainly for overwintering

• *Medicago lupulina* (**Black Medick; Trefoil; Hop Clover; Nonsuch; Yellow Trefoil**): Annual or short-lived perennial, usually prostrate, but can grow 30 cm (12 in) high, with clusters of short-lived yellow flowers. Nitrogen-fixing.
Sowing and harvesting: Sow in late spring or during summer, overwintering plants and then digging them into the soil after about a year.

Medicago lupulina

• *Medicago sativa* (**Lucerne; Alfalfa**): Deep-rooted, upright or spreading perennial, 30–75 cm (1–2½ ft) high; purple flowers are borne in short clusters; nitrogen-fixing.
Sowing and harvesting: Sow mid-spring to mid-summer and overwinter for use during the following year. Plants can be cut down several times to encourage the development of further growth; add the trimmings to a compost heap.

Medicago sativa

Phacelia tanacetifolia

• *Phacelia tanacetifolia* (**Phacelia; Fiddleneck**): Sparse, erect, bristly and fern-like annual; its dense clusters of summer-long, bright blue or lavender-coloured flowers appeal to bees and other insects.
Sowing and harvesting: In mild areas, sow in late summer for overwintering and digging into the soil in early spring. Alternatively, sow in spring for digging into the soil in late summer or early autumn.

• *Secale cereale* (**Rye; Grazing Rye**): Not Rye Grass but an annual cereal type growing 45–60 cm (18–24 in) high; grows rapidly in spring and early summer, developing an extensive root system that is good for the soil's structure, but it prolifically seeds itself and should not be followed by crops of directly sown small plants, such as carrots.
Sowing and harvesting: Sow in late summer and into autumn, to overwinter; it can be dug into the soil towards the end of the following season.

Secale cereale

THE NATURE OF GREEN MANURE PLANTS (CONTINUED)

- *Vicia faba* (**Winter Field Bean; Horse Bean, European Bean; English Bean**): Erect annual, without tendrils, growing 75–90 cm (2½–3 ft) high; it is an agricultural variety of the well-known Broad Bean; if left growing for too long it becomes woody (if this happens, cut down the foliage and place on a compost heap, leaving the plants to resprout with new growth); nitrogen-fixing.

Vicia faba

  Sowing and harvesting: Sow in autumn, overwinter the plants and dig them into the soil during late summer or early autumn of the following year.

- *Vicia sativa* (**Common Vetch; Spring Vetch; Tare; Winter Tare**): Fast-growing annual with a tufted, trailing or sparsely climbing habit, reaching 75–90 cm (2½–3 ft) high; reddish-purple flowers; nitrogen-fixing.
  Sowing and harvesting: Sow in late summer for overwintering and digging into the soil about three months later (early spring). Alternatively, sow in spring or early summer and dig into the soil in late summer or autumn.

Vicia sativa

Plants for growing in spring and summer

- *Fagopyrum esculentum* (syn. *Polygonum fagopyrum*; **Buckwheat**): Little-branched annual with deep roots and red stems; important honey plant, with heads of pink or white flowers.
  Sowing and harvesting: Sow in late spring to mid-summer and dig into the soil in autumn or early winter.

- *Lupinus angustifolius* (**Annual Lupin; Bitter Lupin**): Small, slender-stemmed, hairy annual, growing to about 50 cm (20 in) high; blue flowers during summer; nitrogen-fixing.
  Sowing and harvesting: Sow in late spring or early summer and dig into the soil in autumn or early winter.

Lupinus angustifolius

- *Sinapis alba* (**White Mustard**): Tender, fast-growing annual with a slender tap root and erect, branching stems 30–60 cm (1–2 ft) high; vanilla-scented, golden-yellow flowers in summer.
  Sowing and harvesting: Sow from late spring to the early part of late summer, and dig into the soil in autumn or early winter.

Sinapis alba

- *Trifolium incarnatum* (**Crimson Clover; Italian Clover**): Hairy annual growing up to 50 cm (20 in) high; crimson, pink or pale cream flowers during summer; nitrogen-fixing.
  Sowing and harvesting: Sow from mid-spring to mid-summer and dig into the soil in autumn or early winter. Alternatively, sow in late summer or early autumn and overwinter the plants for digging into the soil during the following season.

Trifolium incarnatum

Trigonella foenum-graecum

- *Trigonella foenum-graecum* (**Fenugreek; Greek Clover; Greek Hay**): Tender, fast-growing, bushy annual with very small, off-white flowers during summer and a mass of green, finger-like leaves.
  Sowing and harvesting: Sow in late spring to mid-summer, and dig into the soil during autumn or early winter.

What are seed and potting composts?

How are they different from garden compost?

Seed and potting composts are specially prepared growing composts, in which you can sow seeds and grow established plants. They are well aerated, and retain moisture yet drain freely. Like soil in a garden, they form a secure base for roots to support seedlings and plants. They provide enough nutrition for the initial growth of seedlings, as well as for the development and continued growth of plants in indoor pots and outdoor containers.

WHY IS THERE A NEED FOR SPECIAL COMPOSTS?

Until the 1930s, each plant nursery and nearly every gardener had their own recipes for making composts in which seeds could be sown and plants grown. They were usually varied, both through tradition and the nature of the loam, the proportions of the ingredients and fertilizers they contain. Also, the loam was often full of weed seeds, diseases and pests. With the increased interest in the early 1900s for raising and growing plants in pots indoors and in containers outdoors, there was a need for standardized composts with an assured quality and suitable for a wide range of plants.

WHAT DO COMPOSTS PROVIDE FOR PLANTS?

There are several fundamental requirements of a seed or potting compost:
- To create a secure base in which seeds can germinate and established plants in pots and other containers can grow.
- To be well aerated to encourage the growth of roots and the activities of beneficial organisms in the compost.
- To retain moisture, but not become waterlogged.
- To provide food for seedlings and plants. Initially, seedlings require very little nutrition, but they grow rapidly and then need a balanced diet. Plants when initially potted or repotted must be given adequate food if their growth is to continue unchecked.

Pest- and disease-free composts are essential when you are growing plants in containers or raising seedlings.

ARE THERE MANY TYPES OF COMPOST?

There are several composts to consider and each has its advantages and disadvantages.

- **Loam-based composts:** Traditional compost, mainly formulated on loam, with the addition of coarse sand or grit and sphagnum moss peat. Fertilizers are also added. Loam-based composts are described on pages 60–61, together with details of making them. However, the continued use of loam (which has a variable nature) is being questioned and there is now a move towards composts that are free from both loam and peat.

- **Peat-based composts:** In earlier times, these were popular (they still have their devotees) and widely used, but the use of peat on a large scale has resulted in the destruction of peat beds, which are home to many animals, birds and insects. For this reason, there has been a radical move towards 'peat-free' or 'reduced-peat' composts.

Advantages of loam-based potting composts

When you are growing plants indoors or in pots and other containers outdoors, loam-based potting composts have a number of advantages:

• They are heavier than peat-based types and therefore able to provide greater stability for large plants.

• They are unlikely to dry out as rapidly or as completely as peat-based composts.

• They contain a larger reserve of minor and trace plant foods than peat-based types.

• They are ideal for most houseplants, but the loam must have been partially sterilized to ensure that pests and diseases are not present.

Note: Loam-based potting composts are best used in conjunction with clay pots.

• **Genie™ composts:** These composts are a more recent development and have been formulated in conjunction with the world-famous John Innes Foundation to produce a totally peat- and loam-free compost. They are sold solely under the trade mark Genie™ and can be used for seed sowing, taking cuttings, potting and growing plants in containers. The main ingredients are composted plant residues and forestry products, such as bark. The production of this compost is sustainable, since it does not contain loam, peat or synthetic chemicals.

DOES ONE COMPOST SUIT ALL PLANTS?

Most composts, whether 'loam-based', 'peat-free', 'reduced-peat', 'peat-based' or Genie™ types, can be used for plants grown in indoors and in containers on patios. However, plants such as orchids, bulbs that are grown for flowering indoors, bromeliads and insectivorous plants need special composts (see pages 66–71 for indoor plants, and pages 72–77 for outdoor plants in containers).

Advantages of peat-based potting composts

When used for growing plants indoors and in containers on patios, peat-based composts have several advantages:

• They are relatively light in weight and therefore easy to carry home from a shop, garden centre or nursery.

• They are more uniform than soil-based composts (the quality of the loam is often variable).

• They are suitable for most plants, but feeding is needed at an earlier stage than when using loam-based composts.

• They dry out more quickly than loam-based potting composts, and are more difficult to remoisten if watering has been neglected and the compost is very dry.

Note: Peat-based potting composts are best used in conjunction with plastic pots.

Can I make my own compost?

It is possible to make your own loam-based compost, but most of the other types are best bought in sealed bags from garden centres and nurseries. (For making loam-based compost, see pages 60–65.)

Usually, the same potting compost suits many different kinds of houseplant.

Orchids usually require special composts (see page 70).

Patio, greenhouse and conservatory plants need clean compost to ensure healthy growth.

Preparing loam for composts

Is sterilized loam essential?

For compost to be made to the John Innes formulae for seed and potting composts (see pages 62–65), the loam must be partially sterilized. Home-made, loam-based composts are often formed from loam removed from the topsoil in gardens, but this probably contains weed seeds, wireworms, eelworms, fungi and other micro-organisms, as well as larvae of pests that graze on the roots of plants. These can soon kill seedlings and plants.

PARTIALLY OR FULLY STERILIZED LOAM?

If loam is fully sterilized, it becomes lifeless and of no value to plants. All the beneficial organisms in it will be killed, as well as the harmful ones. For example, earthworms are killed at about 54°C (130°F), nitrifying bacteria at around 100°C (212° F), and all life in the loam at 126°C (260°F). Therefore, the loam needs to be only partially sterilized for use in either seed or potting composts.

The traditional way to partially sterilize loam is by steaming, which in theory raises the temperature to 100°C (212°F) but in reality raises it to 82–100°C (180–212°F) (most of the nitrifying bacteria survive). Chemical partial sterilization of loam is possible, but this is not suitable for home gardeners.

Placing small amounts of loam in a domestic oven or microwave oven (see below) to partially sterilize it is possible, but take care that steam or hot metal does not touch your hands or arms.

Always keep young children and family pets away from the containers until they are cool.

HOME STERILIZING OF LOAM

Using steam to sterilize soil at home is possible by buying specialized equipment, but on a small, home-garden scale it is not usually practical. Alternatively, electrical soil sterilizing equipment is available; it is thermostatically controlled for temperatures from 60°C to 93°C (140–200°F). However, on a much smaller scale, there are other methods, including the following.

Using a domestic oven

Break up loam so that it is crumbly and spread it in metal (not plastic) trays about 10 cm (4 in) deep. Cover tightly with aluminium foil and insert a meat thermometer through the foil and into the centre of the tray. Adjust the oven to 82–93°C (180–200°F) and leave for 30 minutes.

Check the thermometer several times to ensure the temperature does not rise above 93°C (200°F). Remove from the oven and allow to cool; leave the aluminium foil in place until the loam has entirely cooled and is needed in the preparation of composts. Do not allow it to become contaminated by placing it near dirty compost.

Using a microwave oven

The amount of loam put into a microwave influences the time taken to partially sterilize it. Do not use metal trays or aluminium foil. Place moist soil in an old, heatproof, kitchen glass bowl and cover with clingfilm (check that it is suitable for use in microwaves). Poke a small hole in the centre of the clingfilm to enable excess steam to escape. Operate the unit at full power: to sterilize 1 kg (2.2 lb) of loam takes about 2½ minutes; 5 kg (11 lb) of loam takes around 7 minutes.

When heating is finished, remove from the microwave but leave the covering in place until the loam is needed.

CAN I USE LEAFMOULD INSTEAD OF PEAT?

In theory, well-decomposed leafmould should be suitable for use instead of peat. However, its nature is variable, and because it is not usually fully decomposed (this takes up to two years) often contains pests and diseases. It also cannot be used as part of a John Innes seed or potting compost. (For creating garden compost from deciduous leaves collected in autumn and later used as a mulch, see pages 10–11.)

CAN I USE GARDEN SOIL INSTEAD OF STERILIZED LOAM?

Garden soil is too variable to use in loam-based seed and potting composts without being partially sterilized. It often contains weed seeds, which might germinate among young seedlings, and it is usually impoverished and with a variable structure.

CAN I STERILIZE A SEED OR POTTING COMPOST WHEN MIXED?

No, it is essential to partially sterilize the loam before it is mixed with sphagnum moss peat and coarse sand or grit, as well as with fertilizers.

WHEN I REPOT A PLANT INTO A LARGE POT, DO I NEED A DIFFERENT COMPOST?

John Innes potting composts are graded from No.1 to No.3 (see pages 64–65). Although the basic constituents (partially sterilized loam, sphagnum moss peat and coarse sand or grit) remain the same, the amounts of fertilizers are increased at each stage to provide nutrients for the plant's future growth and development.

If plants are not given an increasingly nutritious compost when repotted, growth declines and consequently their display will be poor.

As soon as a houseplant fills its pot with roots, it benefits from being repotted into a larger pot and given fresh compost.

Acid-loving plants

The acidity of soil or compost is measured on the pH scale (see page 71). Adding ground limestone to the compost raises the pH to about 6.5, which suits most plants. However, ericaceous plants (those that prefer a slightly acidic compost and are often known as calcifuge plants because they dislike lime) need a specialist compost (see page 65).

Ericaceous plants include shrubs, climbers, bulbs and garden perennials. Here are some of the best-known ericaceous plants:

• *Arctostaphylos* (shrub)

• *Calluna* (shrub)

• *Camellia* (shrub)

• *Daboecia* (shrub)

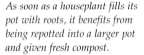

Eucryphia

• *Erica* (shrub)

• *Eucryphia* (shrub)

• *Fothergilla* (shrub)

• *Gaultheria* (shrub)

• *Gentiana* (perennial)

• *Kalmia* (shrub)

• *Lapageria* (climber)

• *Lithospermum* (perennial)

• *Magnolia* (shrub)

• *Nomocharis* (bulb)

• *Pernettya* (shrub)

• *Rhododendron* (shrub)

• *Vaccinium* (shrub)

Making John Innes seed compost

Is this compost easy to make?

The mixing of the ingredients (loam, sphagnum moss peat, coarse sand or grit, chalk and plant foods) that make up John Innes seed compost is simple. However, to ensure success the loam must have been previously partially sterilized to make sure it is free from weed seeds, diseases and soil pests (see pages 60–61). You will need a clean surface on which to prepare it, and dry bags to put it into for storage.

HOW DO THE INGREDIENTS BENEFIT THE COMPOST?

Partially sterilized loam

Sphagnum moss peat

Coarse sand or grit

Superphosphate

Ground limestone

- **Partially sterilized loam:** This forms the main part of the compost, creating a stable base for seedlings. Loam contains essential plant foods, which it releases slowly. It is also valued for the minor plant foods it holds and makes available to seedlings. When preparing loam for use in composts, first put it through a 9 mm (⅜ in) horticultural sieve.
- **Sphagnum moss peat:** This material makes compost more permeable to air and water, improving both its aeration and water-retaining qualities.
- **Coarse sand or grit:** It encourages better aeration in the compost, together with the rapid draining of excess moisture. Because it is a heavy material, it also gives stability to plants in pots, especially when they are large and with a high proportion of leafy growth.
- **Superphosphate:** This contains about 18 per cent phosphoric acid and is needed to encourage root growth in seedlings and until they are moved into John Innes potting compost No.1 (see pages 64–65).
- **Ground limestone:** It corrects acidity in loam, as well as playing an essential role in plant growth.

LOAM-BASED SEED COMPOST

This is how to prepare and mix loam-based seed compost.

1 *Spread out the partially sterilized loam on a clean, flat surface. It should not be wet, as the particles then cling together and it is difficult to mix the ingredients. Preferably, the loam should be slightly dry and friable.*

2 *Spread the sphagnum moss peat on top of the loam. It is usually necessary to first break it up, especially if earlier it has become compressed in a bag through other bags being placed on top of it. If the peat is very dry, water it evenly the day before mixing. This is because very dry peat is later difficult to moisten and may absorb moisture from the loam.*

3 *Spread coarse sand or grit evenly over the peat.*

4 *Mix these three ingredients thoroughly and spread out the mixture to an even depth.*

5 *Dust the ground limestone evenly over the surface, together with the superphosphate, and mix thoroughly (see above right for the amounts of ground limestone and superphosphate of lime to add).*

GETTING THE FERTILIZERS RIGHT

Metric: For each cubic metre of the compost mixture, add:
• 0.6 kg ground limestone.
• 1.2 kg superphosphate of lime.
Imperial: For each cubic yard of the compost mixture, add:
• 1 lb ground limestone.
• 2 lb superphosphate of lime.

CAN I STORE LOAM-BASED COMPOST?

Yes. Place it in strong, sealed, polythene bags in a cool, dry, vermin-proof shed. However, it is best used within a month; if stored for more than two months the compost will become too acid for some plants.

SOWING SEEDS IN SEED-TRAYS (FLATS) IN A GREENHOUSE

Greenhouses provide assured warmth in which seeds can germinate and the subsequent seedlings can grow. After germination, and when the seedlings are large enough to handle, transfer them to seed-trays (flats) containing John Innes potting compost No.1 (see pages 64–65 for details of the compost and pricking off the seedlings). This is essential to prevent them becoming congested, etiolated and susceptible to diseases.

1 Fill a seed-tray (flat) with fresh compost and use your fingers to firm it, especially around the edges. Then refill with compost.

2 Run a straight piece of wood over the top of the tray to remove any excess. Then use a compost presser to firm the surface to 12 mm (½ in) below the rim.

3 Tip a few seeds onto a piece of stiff, folded paper; tap the end to spread the seeds evenly over the compost surface, but not near the edges.

4 Use a flat-based horticultural sieve to cover the seeds with compost to three or four times their thickness. Alternatively, use a culinary sieve, as shown here.

5 To water the compost, stand the seed-tray in a flat-based bowl shallowly filled with water. Remove when the surface is moist. Then cover the tray.

6 Place a sheet of glass (or a transparent plastic 'lid') over the seed-tray (flat). Because condensation forms on the underside, however, you must wipe the glass clear each morning, then invert it so that the dry side is facing the compost. To create a dark environment (needed by most seeds to aid germination), place some newspaper on top of the glass.

Safety first for children

Where children are likely to visit a greenhouse or conservatory to check on recently sown seeds, use a plastic lid rather than a piece of glass to cover the seed-tray (flat).

Making John Innes potting composts

Are there different types?

There are three different potting composts, numbered 1–3, each tailored to the changing demands of plants as they develop and are progressively transferred into larger pots. The basic proportions of partially sterilized loam, sphagnum moss peat and coarse sand or grit remain the same in each compost mixture. The amounts of fertilizers are gradually increased, but the proportion of ground limestone remains the same in each mixture.

WHAT ARE THE BASIC INGREDIENTS USED IN JOHN INNES POTTING COMPOSTS?

These are the same as used for John Innes seed compost (see pages 62–63), although the proportions are different:
• 7 parts partially sterilized loam.
• 3 parts sphagnum moss peat.
• 2 parts coarse sand or grit.
The amounts of fertilizers progressively increase from one compost to the next (see below). Note that the three main parts of all of the composts on these pages and on pages 62–63 are measured by bulk, not weight.

7 parts partially sterilized loam

3 parts sphagnum moss peat

2 parts coarse sand or grit

STORING THE INGREDIENTS

Before being mixed, these materials should always be stored separately in strong, polythene bags in a dry, cool, vermin-proof shed.

John Innes potting compost No.1

Ideal for pricking off young seedlings (see right) or potting up rooted cuttings. The nutrients provide a balanced diet for most young plants.

Metric: For each cubic metre of this potting mixture, add:

• 0.6 kg ground limestone.

• 1.2 kg hoof and horn meal.

• 1.2 kg superphosphate of lime.

• 0.6 kg potassium sulphate (sulphate of potash).

Imperial: For each cubic yard of this potting mixture, add:

• 1 lb ground limestone.

• 2 lb hoof and horn meal.

• 2 lb superphosphate of lime.

• 1 lb potassium sulphate (sulphate of potash).

John Innes potting compost No.2

Used for the general potting of houseplants, as well as other plants when still relatively small but needing a larger pot.

Metric: For each cubic metre of this potting mixture, add:

• 0.6 kg ground limestone.

• 2.4 kg hoof and horn meal.

• 2.4 kg superphosphate of lime.

• 1.2 kg potassium sulphate (sulphate of potash).

Imperial: For each cubic yard of this potting mixture, add:

• 1 lb ground limestone.

• 4 lb hoof and horn meal.

• 4 lb superphosphate of lime.

• 2 lb potassium sulphate (sulphate of potash).

John Innes potting compost No.3

More plentiful in plant foods and used for the final potting of large and mature foliage plants, as well as for large plants in planters both indoors and outdoors. It is ideal for gross-feeding vegetables growing in containers.

Metric: For each cubic metre of this potting mixture, add:

• 0.6 kg ground limestone.

• 3.6 kg hoof and horn meal.

• 3.6 kg superphosphate of lime.

• 1.8 kg potassium sulphate (sulphate of potash).

Imperial: For each cubic yard of this potting mixture, add:

• 1 lb ground limestone.

• 6 lb hoof and horn meal.

• 6 lb superphosphate of lime.

• 3 lb potassium sulphate (sulphate of potash).

John Innes ericaceous compost

This is ideal for plants that dislike lime and prefer a compost that is slightly acid (see page 61). It is formed of:

• 2 parts partially sterilized loam.

• 1 part sphagnum moss peat.

• 1 part coarse sand or grit.

Metric: For each cubic metre of this compost, add:

• 0.6 kg flowers of sulphur.

• 1.2 kg superphosphate of lime.

Imperial: For each cubic yard of this compost, add:

• 1 lb flowers of sulphur.

• 2 lb superphosphate of lime.

PRICKING OFF SEEDLINGS

As soon as the seedlings are large enough to handle, they must be transferred ('pricked off') so that each has more space in which to develop, and an increase in light and air. Seedlings left clustered together become weak and etiolated, and more susceptible to diseases than those with a good circulation of air around them. It is better to transfer seedlings when young, rather than leaving them until large, tough and tightly clustered.

1 *After germination, remove the cover. Whenever the compost shows signs of drying out, water the seedlings by standing the seed-tray (flat) in a bowl shallowly filled with water (see page 63).*

2 *When the seedlings are large enough to handle, water them from below. Then use a small fork to lift a few seedlings and place them on damp newspaper.*

3 *Fill and firm the compost in another seed-tray. Use a small dibber (dibble) to make holes, keeping the outer row 12 mm (½ in) from the sides of the tray.*

4 *Hold a seedling by one of its leaves and insert the roots into a hole (to the same depth as before). Gently firm the compost around the seedlings.*

5 *When the seed-tray is full, gently tap the tray's edges to level any loose compost. Water carefully from above to settle the compost around the roots.*

Potting composts for indoor plants

Do houseplants have special needs?

The range of plants grown indoors, in greenhouses and in conservatories is wide and diverse – from cacti to orchids and bromeliads – and they come from many different climates and soils throughout the world. Some of these plants are terrestrial, living at ground level, and others are epiphytes, growing on the branches of trees where they gain support but are not parasitic. Therefore, a variety of specialist composts is required.

COMPOSTS FOR ALL HOUSEPLANTS

Indoor hanging-basket

Many popular houseplants grow well in John Innes potting composts (see pages 64–65), as well as in 'peat-based', 'peat-free', 'peat-reduced' and Genie™ composts (see pages 58–59). These plants include:

- *Acalypha*
- *Achimenes*
- *Aglaonema*
- *Allamanda*
- *Anthurium*
- *Aphelandra*
- *Ardisia*
- *Aspidistra*
- *Begonia*
- *Bougainvillea*
- *Bouvardia*
- *Browallia*
- *Caladium*
- *Calathea*
- *Calceolaria*
- *Capsicum*

- *Celosia*
- *Chlorophytum*
- *Chrysanthemum*
- *Clerodendrum*
- *Clivia*
- *Codiaeum* (Croton)
- *Coleus* (syn. *Solenostemon*)
- *Crossandra*
- *Cyclamen*
- *Dieffenbachia*
- *Dracaena*
- *Episcia*
- *Euphorbia pulcherrima*
- *Exacum*
- x *Fatshedera*
- *Fatsia*
- *Ficus*
- *Fittonia*
- *Fuchsia*
- *Gloriosa*
- *Grevillea*
- *Hedera*
- *Hoya*
- *Hydrangea*
- *Ixora*
- *Jacaranda*
- *Justicia* (syn. *Beloperone*)
- *Kalanchoe*
- *Leea*
- *Lilium*
- *Maranta*
- *Monstera*
- *Ophiopogon*
- *Oplismenus*
- *Pachystachys*
- *Pandanus*
- *Pelargonium*
- *Peperomia*
- *Philodendron*
- *Pilea*

- *Plumbago*
- *Primula*
- *Saintpaulia*
- *Sansevieria*
- *Saxifraga*
- *Schefflera*
- *Schizanthus*
- *Senecio* (syn. *Cineraria*)
- *Solanum*
- *Soleirolia* (syn. *Helxine*)
- *Spathiphyllum*
- *Streptocarpus*
- *Tolmiea*
- *Torenia*
- *Tradescantia*
- *Yucca*

Floor-standing palm

Influence on watering frequency

Because composts vary from loam-based to peat-free types, their ability to retain moisture or to allow excess water to drain away varies too. Therefore, take care when changing from one compost to another.

INDOOR BONSAI

These miniaturized plants, which grow in relatively small amounts of compost in shallow containers, are created from tropical and subtropical woody plants. Most are grown for their attractive foliage and a few, such as bougainvilleas, for their beautiful flowers. These plants come from diverse places and therefore, depending on their native areas, need special composts. In general, there are three compost mixtures, and each is formed of various combinations of partially sterilized loam, sphagnum moss peat and granite grit.

An instant guide to bonsai composts

Mixture 1
Basic mixture that suits most bonsai.
• 1 part partially sterilized loam.
• 2 parts sphagnum moss peat.
• 2 parts granite grit.

Mixture 2
Especially free-draining mixture and ideal for bonsai native to woodland areas.
• 1 part partially sterilized loam.
• 1 part sphagnum moss peat.
• 3 parts granite grit.

Mixture 3
Essential for bonsai that dislike lime in the compost.
• 1 part partially sterilized loam.
• 3 parts sphagnum moss peat.
• 1 part granite grit.
Note: The various parts of these composts are mixed by bulk, not weight. Always use a clean container to measure them.

Mixing bonsai composts
• It is essential that the compost mixing area is clean.
• All ingredients should be dry when mixed and passed through a sieve to give a particle size up to 5 mm (³⁄₁₆ in). However, too many fine particles clog up the compost, preventing aeration and drainage.

Fig tree (Ficus spp.) grown as a bonsai specimen

Olea europaea (Common Olive)

Proprietary bonsai mixtures
In addition to the bonsai composts outlined above, proprietary compost mixtures are available. These are sold in small amounts and are ready for immediate use or within a couple of months. Store them in a cool, dry, pest-free shed.

BROMELIADS

Bromeliads encompass a wide range of plants, some epiphytic (living on trees for support, but not parasitic) and some terrestrial (living at ground level). They are often native to humid and tropical regions, but are also found in scrubby desert.

With the exception of the 'atmospheric' *Tillandsia* species (Air Plants; see below), most bromeliads can be grown in pots. However, tillandsias that can be grown in pots include *T. cyanea*, *T. grandis*, *T. lindenii* and *T. punctulata*.

Many bromeliads have leaves that form watertight urns at their centres, which hold rainwater together with decayed plant and animal remains that provide nutrition for the plant. Because these plants obtain most of their moisture and food requirements through an 'urn', they usually have small roots (their main purpose is to anchor the plant).

Bromeliads grow well in small pots and, therefore, large amounts of compost are not needed. When potting, check that plants are not potted deeply to ensure the crown of the plant or bases of the leaves are slightly above the compost to prevent decay through being constantly wet.

Compost for bromeliads
The compost for bromeliads growing in pots needs to be well aerated, yet both moisture-retentive and free-draining. Several compost mixtures are recommended, including:

Bromeliads are richly diverse – many have colourful bracts and flowers

- 1 part sharp sand and 1 part osmunda fibre.
- 1 part sharp sand and 1 part peat, with the addition of perlite or forest bark.
- 2 parts peat and 1 part sharp sand or grit.
- Proprietary bromeliad compost.

Whatever the type of compost, it needs to be pH neutral or slightly acid (see page 71). To ensure good drainage, fill the base of the pot with crocks (broken clay pots).

Tillandsia spp. (Air Plants)
These are 'atmospheric' plants that appear to grow with only the benefit of air. Perhaps the best known species is *T. usneoides* (Spanish Moss; Old Man's Beard), which festoons trees and telegraph wires in its native southeastern USA. This species, as well as *T. baileyi*, *T. circinnata*, *T. geminiflora* and *T. ionantha*, can be grown by gluing the plants to shells and decorative pieces of wood. Their care is easy and involves frequent mist-spraying, providing high temperatures, positioning in good, indirect light and misting with a quarter-strength general fertilizer every 3–4 weeks from spring to late summer. No potting is needed.

BULBS GROWN INDOORS

When bulbs are grown in pots and bowls for flowering indoors, there are two main choices of compost:

- John Innes potting compost No.2 (see page 64).
- Bulb fibre, a fibrous, well-drained yet moisture-retentive mix of peat, oystershell and horticultural charcoal. It is ideal for pots with or without drainage holes.

After flowering indoors
If, after flowering indoors, you intend to plant the bulbs in a garden border or to naturalize them in grass, it is best to use John Innes potting compost No.2 or other loam-based composts during the indoor phase. This is because bulbs grown in loam-based compost will flower during the following year when planted in a garden, whereas if they

have initially been grown in bulb fibre it will take a year or so for them to produce flowers after being planted outdoors.

Naturalizing daffodils
When planting daffodil bulbs in informal lawns, use a bulb-planter. This takes out a core of soil and turf, under which a bulb can be planted. Replace the core of soil and turf over the bulb.

CACTI AND OTHER SUCCULENTS

The essential requirement of a cactus compost is to be free-draining and so prevent the roots and base of the plant becoming damaged by excessive moisture, especially during winter. Several composts produce good results, including:

• 4 parts loam-based potting compost and 3 parts sharp sand or grit.
• 2 parts loam-based compost and 1 part sharp grit.
• Proprietary cactus and succulent compost, which is sold by garden centres and specialist cacti and succulent nurseries.

Agave americana 'Variegata'

FERNS

These vary in nature, but the majority of ferns grown indoors need a well-drained compost that retains moisture. Several compost recipes have proved to give satisfactory results, and these include:

• Proprietary fern composts; if, after some experience of them, they appear to retain excessive amounts of moisture, add about one-third extra sharp sand or grit when potting further ferns. (Always keep a note of the compost mixture used, and how well ferns grow in it.)

• 1 part John Innes potting compost No.1, 1 part coarse sand or grit and 2 parts peat.
• 1 part John Innes potting compost No.1 and 1 part sphagnum moss. Because this is especially moisture-retentive, add horticultural charcoal to keep it 'sweet'.

CYCADS

Historically, these are among the earliest seed-bearing plants and were more common in prehistoric times than now. Although they look similar, they are not related to palms. Cycads are mainly native to tropical and subtropical regions, with only a few of them grown in temperate climates as house or conservatory plants.

The most popular species for homes and conservatories is *Cycas revoluta* (Sago Palm), but there are many others. These include other *Cycas* spp., *Dioön caputoi*, *D. edule*, *Encephalartos lehmannii* and *E. senticosus*. Cycads that naturally live in low-light conditions are especially suitable for growing indoors and in conservatories in temperate climates.

Most cycads like a gritty, free-draining soil, and this needs to be replicated when they are grown in a container. Equal parts loam-based compost and sharp grit is ideal, with the base of the container well crocked with broken pieces of clay pots. These plants can live for many years in the same container if it does not constrict the roots.

Cycas revoluta (Sago Palm)

INSECTIVOROUS PLANTS

Sometimes known as insectivores or carnivorous plants, nature has adapted them to live in places where their roots cannot gain sufficient nutrients from the soil. Instead, adaptations allow them to trap and digest insects. They are native to many inhospitable and extreme climates, including dry and aquatic conditions. However, most live in damp, acidic and boggy environments and the following compost mixtures are suitable:

• I part river sand (thoroughly washed), I part non-enriched peat and I part fine perlite (sterile, inorganic material which comes from vitreous rock and provides aeration in the compost). Leave the compost to stand for a couple of weeks before use.
• I part river sand (thoroughly washed) and I part non-enriched peat, thoroughly mixed and allowed to stand for two weeks before use.

Choosing a pot

When repotting an insectivorous plant, always select a pot that is only slightly larger than the existing container, rather than one that is much larger. Also remember that, although clay pots have greater porosity than plastic ones, eventually the inner walls will accumulate salt deposits which gradually cause harm to insectivorous plants.

ORCHIDS

There are two basic types of orchid and this influences the compost that suits them. Terrestrial orchids grow at ground level and are rooted in the soil. Epiphytic types grow on trees and shrubs, but are not parasitic. They only use trees and shrubs for support and anchorage, growing on dead plant debris which collects in the angles of branches and provides moisture and nourishment.

The range of orchids is wide, but the home gardener is usually restricted to those that are relatively easy to grow and suitable for growing indoors (although they will also thrive in greenhouses and conservatories). Orchids suitable for growing indoors, together with composts that suit them, include:

Phalaenopsis 'Alice Girl'

• **Cymbidiums:** Free-draining compost is essential, formed of 2 parts fibrous peat (with a pH of 6.2) and I part coarse perlite. It is also advantageous to add shredded bark to the mixture.
• **Miltonias:** Free-draining compost is essential, formed of 2 parts fibrous peat (with a pH of 6.2) and I part coarse perlite. Shredded bark can be added to the mixture.
• **Odontoglossums:** Use a compost formed of 2 parts fibrous peat (with a pH of 6.2) and I part coarse perlite. It is also possible to add shredded bark to the mixture. An alternative is an equal parts mixture of sphagnum moss and perlite.

• **Paphiopedilums:** Use a well-aerated and free-draining compost, such as 2 parts fibrous peat (with a pH of 6.2) and I part coarse perlite. Sometimes, shredded bark is added to the mixture. Alternatively, you can use a compost that is formed of 3 parts sphagnum moss and I part coarse perlite.
• **Phalaenopsis:** Use a well-aerated and free-draining compost, such as 2 parts fibrous peat (with a pH of 6.2), I part coarse perlite and I part shredded bark. Also add a small

amount of horticultural charcoal. Alternatively, use a compost formed of shredded bark and chopped sphagnum moss.
• **Zygopetalums:** A free-draining and well-aerated compost is essential. Use a mixture of 2 parts fibrous peat (with a pH of 6.2) and I part coarse perlite. Another good compost is 3 parts sphagnum moss, I part coarse perlite and I part shredded bark.

ORCHIDS (CONTINUED)

Other orchid composts to consider

There are lots of orchid composts and this can appear bewildering to new orchid hobbyists, but it need not be a problem. Essentially, when buying an orchid, ask about the compost it is growing in. Then ask if you can buy a small amount of the compost, so that it is to hand when the orchid needs to be repotted. In addition to proprietary orchid composts, the following can be used:

- bark-based compost.
- 3 parts sphagnum moss, 1 part coarse perlite and 1 part shredded bark.
- 1 part rockwool (absorbent type) and 1 part polyurethane foam.
- sphagnum moss and coarse perlite.
- chopped coconut husk.

After a few years, you may wish to experiment with other compost mixtures, but remember that the frequency of watering is influenced by the nature of the compost. Also, you must always ensure that the compost is clean and cannot become contaminated with pests while it is being stored.

What is pH?

This is a scale that shows the degree of alkalinity or acidity in compost or soil. The scale ranges from 1 to 14. A pH of 7.0 is neutral, with figures below that indicating increasing acidity, and those above greater alkalinity (chalkiness). An assessment of pH in compost (or in garden soil) can be made using a pH chemical testing outfit. With this method, an assessment of colour is needed to indicate the pH. Alternatively, some pH testers consist of a probe that you insert into the compost; this is ideal for gardeners who are red/green colour-blind.

Orchids require slightly acid compost, with a pH ranging from 6.0 to 6.5, but usually 6.2. It is possible to influence the pH of compost by adding ground limestone.

Creating humidity

Most orchids prefer to grow in a humid atmosphere, and this can be encouraged by mist-spraying the foliage (not the flowers) each morning. Preferably, all moisture should have evaporated by evening. Alternatively, stand the pot on pebbles in a shallow tray filled with water. Ensure that the base of the pot is not in water.

PALMS

Increasingly, these dramatic plants are grown indoors and in conservatories. They include fan types, with spreading segments, and range from *Trachycarpus fortunei* (Windmill Palm) and *Chamaerops humilis* (European Fan Palm) to *Livistona chinensis* (Chinese Fan Palm).

Fishtail palms are very distinctive and these include *Caryota mitis* (Burmese Fishtail Palm) and *C. urens* (Wine Fishtail Palm).

There are many feather palms, with central leaf-stalks from which leaflets cluster and grow. *Chamaedorea elegans* (syn. *Neanthe bella*; Parlour Palm), *Phoenix canariensis* (Canary Date Palm) and *P. roebelenii* (Pygmy Date Palm) are examples.

Cane types, with reed-like stems, include *Chamaedorea seifrizii* (Reed Palm) and *Chrysalidocarpus lutescens* (Areca or Butterfly Palm).

Many compost mixtures for palms are recommended and some are so complex that the ingredients would be difficult to buy. Therefore, choose one of the following:

- John Innes potting compost No.2 or No.3, with extra coarse sand or grit. This will form a firm base for the often large fronds, as well as providing a compost rich in food. Ensure that the container has several layers of broken clay pots in its base to enable excess moisture to drain freely.
- A proprietary compost mixture specially tailored for palms.

Caryota mitis (Burmese Fishtail Palm)

Outdoor plants in containers

Do I really need special compost?

The main consideration for all composts used to grow plants in containers outdoors is that they should be free from pests and diseases. They should also be uniform in quality and content, both within the bag (if shop-bought, rather than mixed yourself) and from one season to another. Good results from a particular compost in one year will encourage you to use it again the next, but if it is not uniform you will get disappointing results.

WHAT DO COMPOSTS DO FOR OUTDOOR PLANTS IN CONTAINERS?

Similarly to plants grown indoors in containers, composts for outdoor container plants have several roles.

- **Providing a secure base:** Annual plants, such as many summer-flowering bedding plants in windowboxes, troughs and hanging-baskets, do not need the long-term physical support that is essential for shrubs, trees and woody climbers in tubs and large pots. Therefore, the nature of the composts they require is different.
- **Ensuring aeration and moisture retention yet good drainage:** To function properly, roots need to breathe, but at the same time they require moisture (but not waterlogged conditions). Achieving a balance between these needs is not easy. Aquatic plants, of course, have different needs.

- **Providing food for initial growth and later development:** The need for food depends on a plant's longevity, as well as its nature. Bulbs, for example, are powerhouses of stored energy and some, such as hyacinths, can even be grown and flowered without the benefit of compost. Most plants, however, need a balanced diet throughout their lives and this is supplemented by regular feeding during their growing periods.
- **Ensuring that roots have a pest- and disease-free environment:** If pests and diseases are present, plants are soon damaged.

HERBACEOUS PERENNIALS

These are moderately long-term plants, although every 3–4 years they will benefit from division – remove the plant from the container, divide it up into sections each with a good root system, and replant the sections.

When dividing herbaceous perennials, only replant or pot up young parts from around the outside of the clump. Discard the old and woody parts at the clump's centre.

Plant them in a loam-based compost, such as John Innes potting compost No.2 or No.3. This provides a secure base, especially when they are in relatively small containers and have a large amount of foliage. Always place a thick layer of crocks (broken clay pots) in the container's base to ensure that winter rains do not waterlog the compost.

Liatris spicata (Blazing Star)

COMPOSTS FOR HANGING-BASKETS

There are several choices of compost, including these three:

- **Proprietary hanging-basket compost;** some include moisture-retention additives that assist in keeping the compost moist during hot weather.

- Peat-based composts; these are better than loam-based types for use in hanging-baskets, because they are lighter and retain more moisture. However, if the compost becomes dry it is difficult to remoisten them.

- 1 part loam-based compost and 1 part peat-based compost; this is a good compromise – the peat retains moisture and the loam provides food over a long period. Moisture-retentive additives can also be used if regular watering is a problem.

COMPOSTS FOR WINDOWBOXES

The type of compost used depends on the nature of the plants and their display seasons.

- **Spring-flowering displays:** Use well-drained, loam-based compost. This gives a firm base that suits spring-flowering bulbs, biennials and, sometimes, a few small conifers and trailing, small-leaved, variegated ivies.
- **Summer-flowering displays:** A wide range of composts suits these plants, including loam-based, peat-based, peat-free and reduced-peat types, as well as Genie™ composts. Peat-based types retain moisture better than loam-based ones.
- **Winter displays:** Use well-drained, loam-based compost for these long-term displays, which are mainly formed of miniature, slow-growing conifers, trailing variegated ivies and small, evergreen shrubs. This helps to ensure that winter winds and rain do not disturb the plants.

A striking display of petunias

HANGING-BASKETS IN LOBBIES AND PORCHES

The compost you will need in this situation varies, depending on how the plants are to be put into the hanging-basket.

- Where pots are removed, so that plants are planted directly into compost, use a peat-based, peat-free, reduced-peat or Genie™ compost. To assist in moisture retention, add some clay granules to the compost.

- If plants are left in their pots, which are then positioned in an indoor hanging-basket, pack moist peat around them to keep their compost moist and cool, especially when they are in a warm and sunny position.

Drip-trays
Check that a drip-tray is fitted to the basket's base to ensure that water does not drip onto the floor.

Ideal for a rustic porch

WALL-BASKETS AND MANGERS

The choice of compost depends on the situation:

- Use peat-based, peat-free, reduced-peat or Genie™ composts in wall-baskets planted with summer-only flowering plants. However, for spring displays (bulbous plants and spring-flowering biennials) use a well-drained, loam-based compost.
- In large mangers, a mixture of equal parts loam-based and peat-based compost gives good results, especially when the compost is left in the container for several years.
- When planting a small wall-basket, add moisture-retaining materials to the compost.

An ornate, wire-framed wall-basket

COMPOSTS FOR A SINK GARDEN

Stone, glazed or hypertufa sinks become homes to long-lived alpine and rock-garden plants, as well as miniature bulbs and small conifers. They therefore need well-drained, loam-based compost combined with extra sharp sand (to ensure good drainage) and peat (for moisture retention). This mixture suits most plants in stone sinks; if you are planting lime-hating plants, however, buy a special proprietary mixture for acid-loving plants.

You should position the sink on four bricks (one at each corner) to ensure that the drainage holes in the base do not become blocked. This also helps to prevent slugs and snails reaching the plants.

Small border plants and herbs in a stone sink

COMPOSTS FOR TROUGHS

These resemble windowboxes, but are usually positioned either at ground level or displayed on brackets secured to walls. They are also ideal for positioning near to the edge of a balcony, so that plants can trail freely through the railings.

- **Summer-flowering displays:** These need a compost that retains moisture, even when in strong and direct sunlight. Use a peat-based, peat-free, reduced-peat or Genie™ type. Be prepared to feed and water the plants regularly throughout the summer months.

- **Spring-flowering displays:** Mainly comprising spring-flowering bulbs and biennials, they grow best in a loam-based compost. Ensure it is free-draining.
- **Perennial plants:** Use well-drained, loam-based compost for long-term plants. Add extra sharp sand to the mixture to ensure good drainage.

RAISED BEDS

These are permanent features, constructed with a surface that is 23–30 cm (9–12 in) or more above the surrounding ground. They are ideal growing areas when the surrounding soil is extremely acid or alkaline, or drainage is a problem. Usually, these areas are too large for loam-based composts to be used.

Well-drained soil is essential and a mixture of clean, weed-free and pest-free topsoil is suitable; add a generous amount of sharp sand. Make sure surplus water drains away by forming a thick layer of clean rubble in the base, as well as leaving 'weeping holes' around the sides from which water can escape.

An attractive, L-shaped raised bed

SHRUBS AND TREES IN TUBS

A firm, secure and long-term base for their roots is essential if trunks, stems and foliage are to grow safely for several years. Therefore, select a loam-based compost such as John Innes potting compost No.2 or No.3.

Some long-term plants dislike lime and therefore need a slightly acid compost (see page 65 for details of making an ericaceous compost).

If the container into which a long-term plant is to be potted is large, there is always the temptation to use garden soil. If, for cost reasons, this becomes necessary, you should at least first carefully sieve the soil to remove large and obvious pests. Position the tub on three strong bricks. This helps to prevent snails and slugs reaching the plants, as well as enabling hands to be placed under the container if it needs to be lifted and positioned elsewhere.

BULBS IN TUBS

When planting large, golden-faced, trumpet *Narcissus* spp. (Daffodils) in tubs, they can be placed in single or double layers. Use loam-based potting compost. Put each tub on bricks to improve drainage and enable it to be moved easily.

Position bulbs about 36 mm (1½ in) apart

Two layers

Thick layer of coarse drainage material

HERB PLANTERS

Herbs can remain in planters for several years, until they outgrow the container.
• Place a clean planter on three bricks (for improved drainage) in its display position.
• Form a layer of large pebbles in the base. Roll a piece of wire-netting to form a 7.5 cm (3 in) wide tube.

Position it in the centre of the planter with its base resting on the pebbles. Then fill it with pebbles.
• Fill the bottom of the planter with loam-based potting compost until the compost surface is level with the lowest planting hole. Push the roots of a plant through, firm and add more compost until level with the next planting hole. Continue planting in the same way until the sides have been planted.
• When planting the sides is complete, a few plants can be planted in compost at the top of the planter.
• Lastly, thoroughly water the compost to settle it around the roots.

COMPOST FOR WATER PLANTS

Aquatic plants should always be planted in individual, plastic-mesh containers; never put them directly into soil in the pond's base because the roots could damage the pond's construction or waterproof liner, and it will also be very difficult to remove them if necessary.

The best compost is a heavy loam that has been enriched with a sprinkling of bonemeal to encourage rapid root development. Ensure that the loam is free from decaying debris, such as old roots. After planting, add a layer of clean pea-shingle on top of the loam to prevent it being disturbed by fish and then clouding the water.

TOMATOES IN GROWING-BAGS

Growing-bags contain peat-based compost with the addition of fertilizers. Plant three cordon-type (single, upright stems) in a standard growing-bag. Supports are essential – proprietary metal types are available, but home-made ones fashioned from bamboo canes and wires are possible. In a greenhouse, it is possible to push the bamboo canes through the bag's base to make them more secure. This has the bonus of ensuring that surplus moisture can escape from the bag.

POTATOES IN GROWING-BAGS

Potatoes can be grown in peat-based compost in growing-bags.

• In early to mid-spring, prepare a growing-bag by thoroughly shaking it to loosen the compost. Place the bag on a patio or pallet and cut eight equally spaced 7.5 cm (3 in) long cross-slits in the top. Do not cut away any of the plastic bag. If the compost is dry, water it thoroughly through the slits.

• Into each slit, push one healthy tuber of an early potato variety, so that it is near the base of the growing-bag and covered with compost.
• Fold back the slits to ensure that light is excluded.
• Regularly check that the compost is moist, but be careful not to add too much water.
• Shoots will arise through the slits; if there is any risk of frost, cover them at night with newspaper.

• When you are ready for an early crop of young potatoes, pull back one of the slits and harvest the tubers.
• There is no need to harvest all the potatoes at the same time; fold back the plastic, especially if frost is forecast; it is also essential to exclude all light from the tubers.

PREPARING A STRAWBERRY BARREL

Because ornamental barrels are long-term features, use well-drained, loam-based compost to which has been added extra sharp sand or grit. Do not use soft sand. Peat-based composts are not suitable, as they tend to compress and, eventually, exclude air and reduce drainage.

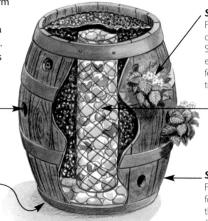

Step 5
Fill the tube with coarse pebbles, then add compost to the level of the lowest hole. Systematically, put a strawberry plant into each hole and add more compost. Put a few strawberry plants in the top. Water the compost.

Step 2
Between the metal bands drill a series of 12–18 mm (½–¾ in) wide holes. Then, use a pad-saw to widen them to about 5 cm (2 in). Smooth the edges of the holes.

Step 4
Roll 2.5 cm (1 in) mesh wire-netting into a tube 10–13 cm (4–5 in) wide, and long enough to stand on pebbles in the base and rise to just below the barrel's top.

Step 1
Turn the barrel upside down and drill 18–25 cm (¾–1 in) wide drainage holes in the base. Check that the timbers are strong enough to support compost.

Step 3
Position the barrel upright and place on four stout bricks. Check that the top of the barrel is level; fill the base with 10–15 cm (4–6 in) of large pebbles.

GROWING BAMBOOS IN CONTAINERS

It is possible to grow bamboos in garden soil in containers, but this exposes roots to the dangers of pests. Instead, use an equal parts mixture of loam-based potting compost and a peat-based or peat-free type. The peat-based type increases the compost's ability to retain moisture, while the loam-based compost creates greater stability for tall bamboos, as well as providing long-term plant foods.

Small bamboos for containers

• *Pleioblastus pygmaeus* (Dwarf Fern-leaf Bamboo)
• *Pleioblastus variegatus* (Dwarf White-striped Bamboo)
• *Pleioblastus viridistriatus* (Golden-haired Bamboo)

Pleioblastus variegatus (Dwarf White-striped Bamboo)

CLIMBERS IN TUBS AND LARGE POTS

Where annual climbers are growing in small pots, they are best put in a moisture-retentive compost such as a peat-based, peat-free, reduced-peat or Genie™ type. However, when long-term climbers (herbaceous and those with a woody framework) are grown in tubs and large pots, it is better to use an equal parts mixture of peat-based compost and a loam-based type. This will provide long-term stability, as well as nutrition.

Herbaceous climber for a tub

• *Humulus lupulus* 'Aureus' (Yellow-leaved Hop): support with a tripod of long canes inserted into compost in the tub.

Passiflora caerulea (Common Passion Flower)

GROWING APPLES IN TUBS AND LARGE POTS

Apples are popular tree or bush fruits for containers on a patio, but there are a few essential considerations. It is vital to use wooden tubs or large terracotta pots, about 38 cm (15 in) deep and wide. Place broken pieces of clay pots in the base and use a loam-based compost. In small gardens or on mini-patios where there is only space for one tree, choose what is known as a 'family tree', which combines several different varieties in one tree.

Glossary

Acid soil Soil which has a pH of less than 7.0 (see pH).

Alkaline soil Soil which has a pH above 7.0 (see pH).

Annual weeds Weeds that complete their growing cycle, from the germination of seeds to the production of flowers, in a single season. They can be added to compost heaps and bins, where they will decompose.

Beneficial insects Insects that act as predators and parasites on garden pests.

Bulb fibre Fibrous, well-drained yet moisture-retentive mixture of peat, oyster shell and horticultural charcoal, used for growing indoor bulbs, such as hyacinths.

Compost bin Receptacle for compost (see page 28).

Compost heap Traditional way to compost organic garden and kitchen waste, by forming a heap (see page 28) rather than using a bin.

Compost hole Hole used for composting (see page 29).

Compost trench Trench used for composting (see page 29).

Compost tumbler Plastic, drum-like container that can be rotated to encourage garden and kitchen organic waste to decompose rapidly.

Container gardening Growing plants in containers, such as hanging-baskets, wall-baskets, window boxes, pots and tubs.

Container-grown plant Plant that is sold growing and established in a container, ready for planting.

Crocks Pieces of broken clay pots used to cover drainage holes in containers. Preferably, they should be positioned concave-side down.

Digging, double Digging soil to the depth of two spade blades, 50–60 cm (20–24 in). Double digging is usually only undertaken when land is being converted from grass land to a garden plot, or where the land is compacted and the drainage poor.

Digging, single Digging soil to the depth of a spade's blade, 25–30 cm (10–12 in). This is the usual method used for digging and mixing in decomposed vegetable waste, and is performed in late autumn or winter.

Friable Refers to soil that is crumbly and is ideal for sowing seeds or planting plants.

Genie™ compost Relatively new type of multipurpose compost, based on composted plant residues and forestry products, such as bark. Its production is sustainable and does not harm the environment.

Green manuring Growing a crop and later digging it into the soil to improve the structure and increase fertility.

Growing-bag Originally introduced to grow tomatoes on disease-infected soil, but now widely used as homes for many flowering plants, as well as herbs and vegetables. Growing-bags that have been used for one season can, in the following one, be topped up with peat and fertilizers and used again.

Humus Dark brown or black part of soil containing valuable plant foods, resulting from decomposed organic material being added.

John Innes composts Range of composts for seeds and plants developed at the John Innes Horticultural Research Institute (see pages 62–65).

Leafmould Deciduous leaves that are fully decomposed (this takes up to two years).

Loam Natural mixture of fertile soil, sand, clay, silt and decayed organic material.

Loam-based compost Compost primarily based on partially sterilized loam (see pages 60–61).

Nitrogen-fixing plants Some plants (usually leguminous species and with the benefit of certain soil bacteria) are able to convert atmospheric nitrogen into nitrogen stored in nodules on their roots (see pages 54–55).

Organic mulching Forming a 7.5–10 cm (3–4 in) thick layer of decomposed organic waste over the soil's surface (see page 47).

Organic waste Any waste which comes from plant or animal matter and is decomposable.

Peat Partly decomposed vegetable material, usually acid, that is often used in potting and seed composts. However, the repeated cutting of this material from peat beds destroys the environments of many birds, animals and insects.

Peat-based compost Compost based on peat, with the addition of fertilizers.

Peat-free compost Compost based on non-peat materials, with the addition of fertilizers.

Perennial weeds Weeds that live for 2–3 years or more, often with roots that penetrate deeply into the soil. Such weeds, when dug up and removed, cannot be used on compost heaps or in bins because they are likely to regrow.

Perlite Small granules of expanded volcanic material that are added to composts to improve their aeration.

pH Logarithmic scale that indicates the degree of alkalinity or acidity in compost or soil (see page 71).

Pricking off Initial moving of seedlings from where they were sown in pots or seed-trays (flats) to wider spacings in other seed-trays or pots.

Quick composting Method of composting that encourages organic materials to decompose more rapidly than if on a compost heap or in a compost bin (see pages 30–31).

Reduced-peat compost Compost containing less peat than in peat-based types.

Shredder Electric or petrol-driven machine for shredding woody waste from gardens.

Sp./spp. Abbreviations of 'species' (singular and plural).

Sphagnum moss A type of moss that was widely used in earlier times to line wire-framed hanging-baskets to assist in moisture retention and to prevent compost spilling out of the container.

Subsoil Soil beneath the normal depth at which the ground is cultivated, often heavy and clay-like.

Syn. Abbreviation of 'synonym', used when a plant's botanical name has been changed but the previous name is still widely used.

Topsoil Top layer of soil, in which most plants grow. Partially sterilized topsoil is used in loam-based composts.

Vermicompost Decomposed/digested material resulting from the activities of worms in a wormery.

Vermiculite Lightweight, mica-like material that is added to compost to improve both water retention and aeration.

Vermiculture Use of worms to turn organic kitchen and garden waste into compost.

Wormery Enclosure for turning organic kitchen and garden waste into vermicompost by means of special worms (see pages 48–53).

Index

Acknowledgments

Photographs: Ardisam (page 24BR), Bosch (back of cover and pages 24L and 24CT), Flymo (page 24TR), iStock (pages 2 and 6),
Paul Whittaker (page 77T), Peter Chan (page 67B), Struik (page 67T), The Worm Works (page 50TL) and WormCity (pages 5, 50TR and 50B).
Other photographs by AG&G Books.